The Chinese Prime Minister

A Play in Three Acts

by Enid Bagnold

A Samuel French Acting Edition

SAMUEL FRENCH

FOUNDED 1830

SAMUELFRENCH.COM

THE CHINESE PRIME MINISTER, by Enid Bagnold, was presented by Roger L. Stevens at the Royale Theatre, New York City, January 2, 1964. Setting by Oliver Smith. Costumes by Valentina. Lighting by Jean Rosenthal. Associate producers Lyn Austin, Victor Samrock. Directed by Joseph Anthony.

THE CAST

BENT ....*Alan Webb*
OLIVER ....*Peter Donat*
SHE ....*Margaret Leighton*
ROXANE ....*Joanna Pettet*
ALICE ....*Diane Kagan*
TARVER ....*Douglas Watson*
RED GUS RISKO ....*James Olson*
SIR GREGORY ....*John Williams*

The action takes place in the drawing room of a once fashionable house in London.

ACT ONE
SCENE 1: Late Autumn.
SCENE 2: Early Spring.

ACT TWO
The same evening.

ACT THREE
Five months later.

TIME: Any year in which the actress is sixty-nine. One hour before she is due to leave for the theatre for her evening performance.

PLACE: The drawing room of an old, once-fashionable, house in London; probably on the first floor up.

3

THE SET: A late Georgian window, perhaps a bay window which overlooks what has been successively a stable yard or the Mews Cottage garden. *The window is full of the leaves of a very old plane tree. One can hardly see out of the window and green light filters through.* There is also a window on the street. There are three direct doors, one to Her bedroom, one to the kitchen quarters, one to the hall. But there must in some way be a method of reaching the rest of the house—perhaps by a vestibule seen between columns at one side, so that anyone coming from upstairs can be seen as they go to the hall door.

The Chinese Prime Minister

ACT ONE

SCENE 1

When the CURTAIN goes up: SHE—*the lady of the house—in a dressing gown, is finishing her breathing exercises at the open window* facing the plane tree, in full leaf, *her back to the audience—raising and dropping her arms—while her son,* OLIVER, *counts aloud for her.* OLIVER *is twenty-nine.*

OLIVER. (*Idly—as he reads a book.*) . . . forty-four . . . forty-five . . . forty-six . . .

SHE. (*Impetuously turning.*) Just imagine!—*No description at all!* It shakes me!

OLIVER. Go on. Forty-seven . . .

SHE. (*Coming Downstage, but still moving her arms automatically.*) He just indicates love! . . . (*Breathing.*) leading to marriage . . . —*That's all!*

OLIVER. . . . forty-eight . . . forty-nine . . .

SHE. (*Spitting it out.*) Fifty! This isn't a day when I can breathe! (*Seeing old* BENT *in the doorway.*) *What is it,* Bent!

BENT. Sir Gregory, m'lady—

OLIVER. *What!*

BENT. Your husband again on the telephone. I've switched it up.

SHE. Then switch it down. I don't take calls from unknown men!

OLIVER. (*Impatient.*) Who do you mean by—"Sir Gregory"?—My father's dead.

BENT. (*Imperturbable.*) At the Savoy, he said.

SHE. And I don't take calls from unknown men!

5

OLIVER. (*Casually stretching out an arm to the telephone.*) I'll see what it is—

SHE. (*Sharply urgent.*) *I'll* see! (OLIVER *looks up astonished at her tone. Half-excusing herself.*) I know what it is—it's about a hat. . . . (*He gives telephone to her.*)

BENT. No, it isn't.

SHE. (*Holding* BENT *with her eyes over the telephone.*) Who's speaking? (*To* OLIVER.) Well—don't stand over me! (*He strolls away and listens.*) Ten—what? Ten—*orchids?* (OLIVER *smiles.*) Ten—*DOZEN!* (*Putting her hand over the telephone she holds it away from her a moment. Then, suddenly.*) I wish they *were* for me—but I'm afraid they're not! (*Replaces instrument on stand.*)

OLIVER. Is it love?

SHE. Of course it's love—but he had the wrong number. (*To* BENT.) I'd *forgotten!*—It's your afternoon off!

BENT. (*Grim.*) But it's gone.

SHE. If it's gone you could stay and boil my egg.

BENT. Mr. Oliver said he'd boil it. (*Pulling out his large turnip watch on its chain and consulting it.*) I'm off now.—The gin's running short. It's my young lady—meeting me. (*Obstinate, as he turns to go.*) It *was* Sir Gregory's voice on the telephone.

SHE. So you said yesterday—and it wasn't! (*Reasoning with him.*) Look, Bent! When one gets old—as you and I get old—people long dead— (*But he is going.*)

OLIVER. Take it from me! My father's been dead twenty years.

BENT. I know it. But that doesn't stop him ringing. (*Goes.*)

SHE. (*Carelessly.*) It's an *obsession!* (*Picking up the note again—washing out the subject of* BENT.) Telling me *nothing!* Does Tarver think I like a total surprise!

OLIVER. Tarver hates to be embarrassed. You sent him to school too early.

SHE. I never know anything about him!

OLIVER. He doesn't mean you to.

SHE. I used to.

OLIVER. If you look back—not since he went to school when he was seven.

SHE. Those schools!—Thank God I never sent you!—Settle me, Oliver. (*He arranges the cushions on the sofa.*) My handkerchief. In my bag. Over there. (*Curling up on the sofa.*) And he knows—before the theatre—things upset me! And *tonight!*—The last night of the play!—after twenty-three months— (*Suddenly, conventionally, dropping a small false wreath.*) it's so *sad.*

OLIVER. (*Walking over to the secretary on which lie a pile of those yellowish envelopes that contain scripts. Mocking, over shoulder.*) But you're *glad.*

SHE. (*A conventional rebuke.*) We are loyal to our plays.

OLIVER. (*Holding about six of the heavy envelopes up between his two hands as though weighing them.*) And the next play? What about these?

SHE. I haven't read them. I haven't *opened* them! Those lines—those words! (*Pushing them away as he holds them near her. Touching her forehead.*) I feel a muscle in my forehead that's carried words for forty years! Oh—why does no one write *real* plays—about the fascination and disaster of being old!

OLIVER. What's the fascination?

SHE. What might lie ahead of me! If I had the daring . . .

OLIVER. What's the disaster?

SHE. What you all expect for me! That for me it's the end of surprises! For me it's the final run-in.

OLIVER. It may be the winning post.

SHE. My horse, if it wins, runs past the post into the fog. (*Reverting again, toying with note.*) *Telling me nothing!* Not one word about the girl! Not even a surname! —She's called Alice. That's all!

OLIVER. You can expect she'll be beautiful. That's the prime thing my brother demands in a girl.

SHE. (*Vexedly.*) So do you. (*A door opens.* ROXANE *comes in dressed to go out. Very chic, very young, very lovely—she crosses the room, or the vestibule. They watch* her. *Surely she will speak? Not a word! Giving her every chance. At the last ditch.*) Good morning.

ROXANE. (*Immediately stopping: polite.*) Good afternoon, Mama.

OLIVER. (*Involuntarily.*) How sweet you look!

ROXANE. (*Gravely.*) Thank you. (*Stepping forward as though about to say something of importance.*) Mama . . .

SHE. Yes?

ROXANE. (*With her special good manners.*) I shall be out tonight. (*Goes.*)

SHE. (*A moment's silence.*) "Mama"—as *she* uses it— is like a sword! Her manners are so beautiful they're like an armour! I should like to have seen her as she was being born—exquisitely thanking the doctor!—Do you know where she's going?

OLIVER. No.

SHE. (*Angry.*) You *ought* to know!

OLIVER. *I* ought to? Or is that a general rule?

SHE. *You* ought to!—It's laughable!

OLIVER. Those in love are always laughable.

SHE. She's obviously dining with some man.

OLIVER. She may be.

SHE. Don't you care! She's your wife!

OLIVER. She hates to be asked. It's a kind of adolescence. In a way I understand it.

SHE. Understand her, if you like! But *hide* it!

OLIVER. I'm not that kind of man! I'm not inscrutable!

SHE. It's she who is inscrutable.—She isolates herself from you because you don't try to master her, and she isolates herself from me because she guesses I know it. I thought she could be a daughter. And so she is. But an enemy-daughter! The truth is—that I ought not to be able to watch your troubles as I do! The truth is—you ought never—once you married—to have lived on here with me!

OLIVER. (*Lamely.*) She's not grown up.

SHE. But she will be!

OLIVER. Couldn't you be charitable?

SHE. I could. But I'm not that kind of woman. You

think I've done badly by her? I began by trying hard.
But it's dishonest to make friends with the next generation.

OLIVER. Then what about me?

SHE. You were born when your father left me. You and
I have a language of intimacy.

OLIVER. She knew that. She knew she wasn't elected
to the club!

SHE. You promised you'd bring her last night. The
tickets were waiting.

OLIVER. I know.

SHE. She hasn't seen me play since you were married.—
She avoids my triumphs!—she keeps me in a single focus
—as a mother-in-law! (*Dismissing the subject.*) How
soon will they be here?

OLIVER. Five minutes.

SHE. And *now* what sort of girl is Tarver bringing to
me! Who else do I have to be unselfish for? (*Smiling.*)
I used to look at my daughters-in-law—in their prams in
the Park—and *hate* them! . . . What will—"Alice" be
like?

OLIVER. She'll be at least twenty-five. And sophisticated. A cool, pale, marble girl—and a catch socially.

SHE. Is Tarver a snob?

OLIVER. No, but he doesn't undervalue his world. . . .

(*The door opens.* TARVER *comes in, the elder son, with*
ALICE.)

TARVER. (*Giving* ALICE *a push as she hangs back.*) Go
on, Alice.

(ALICE *is seventeen, a hobbledehoy. Awkward. Hair-
trouble.*)

ALICE. How do you do.

SHE. (*Rising ceremoniously.*) Can I call you Alice?

ALICE. Please do.

SHE. (*Drawing* ALICE *to a chair beside the sofa.*) Sit

here. Let me *look* at you. (*Smiling ravishingly. Taking*
ALICE's *hand.*) I don't kiss you. Things ought to come
gradually! (*Her smile belying her words.*) It's a relationship—of enormous danger—my little girl! (*Putting a
hand up to* TARVER.) I think she ought to have come
alone to see me!

ALICE. (*Eager, blurting.*) That's what I thought, too!
(*With a gulp.*) I've been dying to meet you! (*Another
gulp.*) You've twice signed my little book—did you know?

SHE. *I* have?

ALICE. Once outside the Duchess Theater at the stage
door. Once outside the Haymarket . . .

SHE. You're one of the girls with little books and pen-
cils!

ALICE. I'd never have dared to ask you if Tarver hadn't
come, too!

SHE. (*Bowled over.*) *Tarver!*—I can't believe it! *Tarver,* at the stage door!

TARVER. (*Changing the subject.*) This is Oliver—Alice.

OLIVER. I've seen you somewhere.

ALICE. So have I you. You came down with . . .
(*Rapturously.*) your mother—when she gave the prizes at
school. I got one for gym.

TARVER. (*His hand on her shoulder.*) My *darling!*—
You sound like a goop but I love you!

ALICE. (*To* OLIVER.) I was so envious! You brought
a marvellous girl with you!

OLIVER. That was my wife.

ALICE. (*To* HER.) So you've got a daughter-in-law
already? I couldn't take my eyes off her. She was so well
dressed she made me feel a slob.

TARVER. (*To his* MOTHER.) This is a divine girl but
she takes knowing! I've *done* with all my sleek ideals!
I've remade my taste in girls. This one's *not* my type . . .
(*Puts an arm around* ALICE's *waist.*) She's *not* well
dressed—she's *not* beautiful—but I love her from scratch!
Look at her hair! (*Rumples it:* ALICE *dodges out from
his hand, displeased.*) She's as newborn as a chicken!

SHE. (*Gravely—to* ALICE.) Do you feel so young?

ALICE. (*Carefully.*) Not as young as that. (*Eagerly.*) Will you let me marry him?

SHE. And have my daughter-in-law my fan?

ALICE. Is that against me?

SHE. We won't let it be! (*To* TARVER.) Leave me alone with her. (*To* ALICE.) Will you talk alone with me?

ALICE. Thank you.

TARVER. (*Going to the console table.*) I'll give you both ten minutes. And I'll take a drink with me.

SHE. There's whiskey. And a syphon.

TARVER. (*Holding up bottle.*) There's not much gin!

SHE. (*Looking vaguely round.*) I don't know where it goes . . . *I* never touch it! All the girls get drunk on gin now—in my world.—Put on the egg—Oliver.

TARVER. Is it Bent's day out?

SHE. (*Vexedly.*) Yes, it is. (*To* ALICE.) Bent's my butler. Fifty years my Impresario!—and pokes his nose in too much! (*To* OLIVER.) And one of these days I'm going to retire him! I can't stand his nostalgia another minute!

TARVER. Nostalgia for what?

SHE. Even served at dinner I have to hear it! Nostalgia for girls! *He* wants to get married—too!

TARVER. At his age!—For *girls!*

SHE. He calls all women girls up to sixty. But this one really *is* a girl. (*Pause.*) And much too developed for him!

TARVER. Are you inventing this? Just to feel good at getting rid of him?

SHE. No. This is true.

ALICE. Do you invent things?

SHE. (*Amused.*) If life is annoying I do. (*As* OLIVER *goes to the kitchen door.*) Take Tarver with you.

TARVER. (*Carrying his whiskey. At kitchen door—to* ALICE.) Got courage enough?

ALICE. Yes, thank you.

SHE. (*Getting up—shutting door after* TARVER—*turning to survey her new* DAUGHTER-IN-LAW. *At length.*) This will be like talking from two sides of the world! (*To console table.*) First—you must stop worshipping me just as soon as you can. (*Takes what remains of gin, looks at it, puts it away on another table.*)

ALICE. How does one?

SHE. You may be marrying Tarver because you are infatuated with me.

ALICE. I may be.

SHE. Tarver's my son. But I don't *know* him. I can't help you in dealing with him.

ALICE. Oh, Tarver's easy to know!

SHE. Do you think so? (*Pursuing her own line of thought.*) And then—as you get to know *me* better—you may hate me.

ALICE. Why?

SHE. Because we shall never have been neutral. You have begun by adoring me, and for the wrong reasons. And when you stop adoring me you'll take it out on me. —Don't interrupt!—After that—you may further divide Tarver and me—by complaint of me. (*As ALICE is about to protest. Over-riding.*) I don't say it *will* happen. I say it might. One is sweet to one's daughter-in-law in the first year because one is sucking up to one's son. Quite soon she may become an enemy. In the end there's a chance she may become a friend. No, don't interrupt me! . . . Then there are other complications. (*Turning and facing ALICE.*) I require a great deal of attention. I'm used to it. A woman who is successful on the stage isn't easy. Oliver manages it. But Oliver's the tender one. (*Suddenly remembering—faintly put out.*) I should be having my egg in a few minutes! (*Returning across the room. ALICE just sits and looks at her.*) I suppose you would call me a selfish woman. But self-expression takes doing. Especially on the stage. An actress must be an egotist. Her personality is so important to her! And that's the real truth about people! They are not types. They aren't mothers-in-law and daughters-in-law! They are creatures ardently engaged on themselves! I say all this to show you that you and I have got to stand up to each other.—It won't be roses! (*Walks up and down.*) Another thing . . . (*The TELEPHONE rings. Picks it up.*) Who is speaking?

(*Listens. Smiling.*) Always the same wrong number!
(*Presses instrument to her breast so that it is muffled.*)

ALICE. (*Timidly.*) What other thing?

SHE. I don't want to seem ridiculous. In your eyes no
doubt . . . (*With a half smile she lifts the telephone
from its muffled state and holds it not far from her
mouth.*) But my private life isn't run on age. It may surprise you, Alice, but men still fall in love with me. . . .
(*Puts the telephone back on its stand—touches a flower
in a gilt basket. Takes off card from flowers.*)

ALICE. (*Devoted.*) I should think so!

SHE. Yes, there's a glamour hangs about a woman of
power and success—yes. But that's not exactly what I
mean—what I want! What I'm trying to say—but don't
answer me—is that my life is still full of surprises. I have
an extra vitality and extra expectations! I can't imagine
living on when there are no more expectations!—I don't
know why I say this to you—except that it may be a
revelation for *your* old age! Though by then you will have
forgotten it! Oh, Alice, how young you are! Are you sure
you can be happy with Tarver?

ALICE. Absolutely! He's the kind of man I've always
dreamt of. He's a bully and I love that. I always longed
to marry a bully.

SHE. (*Crumpling card in her hand.*) Then you can understand more than I!— (*Inward smile.*) His father was
a bully.

ALICE. Tarver thinks he can remodel me.

SHE. And can he?

ALICE. No. But I love to see him trying.

SHE. It seems to me that at first sight I underrated
you!

ALICE. Can I ask you one thing?

SHE. (*Cautious.*) It depends.

ALICE. On the whole—and quite apart from difficulties
—do you like me?

SHE. Yes, I do. But don't count on it lasting!

ALICE. I worship you. But I quite see that to worship

you is a kind of puppy-fat. Tarver says—that you criticize him—

SHE. (*Vexed.*) He talks about me!

ALICE. Only with me.—Only because he loves you.

SHE. (*Sarcastic and still hurt.*) Thank you.

ALICE. You don't like my saying that. But you *did* want to know. (*Struggling on.*) As a matter of fact—and to be honest . . .

SHE. Go on.

ALICE. It's a message from him. He says you *don't* know that he loves you. And he wants you to know. (*Hurrying on—afraid of being stopped.*) He wants our marriage to be started like that. With you knowing. So that you would never think . . . (*Choking with difficulty.*) that I had . . . more love than you. I mean— I've not stolen him from you! (*Pause.*) Would you think it fearful cheek—if I warned you? (SHE *is silent because she is thinking of what has been said.*) There are things in me—that you ought to know. I get bursts of rebellion. It's my growing pains. I've got a temper like the devil. I can't cure it. And a sort of mutiny. If you try to push me I go hard and something rushes over me. A terrible obstinacy. I can't help it. And then—what Tarver *doesn't* know—but I'm telling you—is that I mind terribly, terribly—that I look as I do. I could have killed Tarver when he said just now—and in front of you— that I wasn't beautiful. Though I know I'm not.

SHE. (*Absent.*) Oh, but I'll dress you—so that you won't know yourself!

ALICE. (*In dead earnest.*) That's just what I don't want you to do! You're so powerful that you could change me! And I mustn't be changed! It must be *my* business! That's what I used the word "warning" for! I want to warn you to let me do my growing by myself. (*Trying hard to get over what she means.*) If the *wrong* face— looks out of *my* face— (*Breaking off.*) Oh—a girl's looks are *agony!* Do you remember it?

SHE. It seems to me I said the same five minutes ago! But I couldn't have said it—as you do—so clearly!

ALICE. I've got a sort of back-to-the-wallness that makes me clear. (*As the door opens—loud, to* TARVER.) All right! We've made a fist of it.

TARVER. Is that my magical hockey girl?

SHE. Yes, Tarver. And she and I understand everything!—Except that I don't know her name!

ALICE. Alice Feathers.

SHE. *Feathers!*

ALICE. I'm afraid so. And in case you want to know, I have an aunt who drinks. And my father and mother are separated.

TARVER. So were mine.

OLIVER. (*Coming in with the tray.*) The sacred moment has come!

(SHE *sits down on the sofa.*)

TARVER. The moment of the egg. From now on, Alice, my mother is hardly human.

SHE. (*Grave.*) I have to leave in half an hour for the theatre. I always sit alone before I go. The play comes off tonight—and I have to say something.

ALICE. (*With bated breath.*) Make a *speech* . . . to the *audience!*

SHE. I suppose so. I expect so.—Turn off the lights, Oliver.—Except this one.

ALICE. Oh, I wish I could be there!

SHE. You *can* be.—You arrange it, Oliver.—*You'll* be coming?

OLIVER. Well, no.—But I'll ring about a seat for Alice.

ALICE. (*Worshipping.*) When can I see you again?

SHE. (*Smiling.*) When you want to be disloyal to your husband—with his mother! Look in my engagement book, Oliver.

OLIVER. (*Picking up a small scarlet engagement book. Turning pages.*) The whole of next week . . . *full.*

SHE. Not a chink—not a corner for a new daughter!

OLIVER. (*Looking ahead in the book.*) No.—Nor the week after.

SHE. (*Indignant.*) So it has been for forty years! It creeps ahead of me! It strangles me! (*To* ALICE.) I'll ring you! I'll tear a living minute from that book!—Goodbye.—And don't have a moment's doubt, Tarver. I adore her. (TARVER *and* ALICE *go out. To* OLIVER.) I feel in love myself. I feel *included.* I feel . . . (*Looking far away.*) the meal might be for me! (*Reminded of her egg, she attacks it.*)

OLIVER. Don't go too far!

SHE. I thought I would be jealous. And very critical.—And God knows there's room for criticism!—She's a grave pudding of a child. But she won't be a pudding long.

OLIVER. Were you kind?

SHE. Yes, I was kind. But kindness is so fugitive. It comes like a gust into the heart. And blows out again. (*Putting down her spoon and looking up.*) A girl as young as that brings one to one's senses! She looked at me as though she thought I *knew* about life! And I know nothing!—And I play—tonight—that "wise woman" who knows *all* the conclusions! What do I know of a private life! I've been defrauded! . . . I wish I could meet . . . (*Smiling at him.*) a Chinese Prime Minister. (*Pause.*) Before the coming of Christ. In the East—when age was near paradise and not a prison . . .

OLIVER. (*In the same tone—humouring her.*) A Prime Minister still in office?

SHE. No! He makes a triumph of his retirement! He writes poems that will outlive his achievements!—He carries a birdcage. We go up in the mountains together . . . (*Her voice stops.*)

OLIVER. . . . . very faintly etched on the landscape . . . Is it love?

SHE. Of course! And why not—why shouldn't it be! (BENT *comes in but she pays no attention.*) I suppose the car is round—and my big coat in the hall? (*As* OLIVER *goes.*) Call me in fifteen minutes and I'll start. (*As the door shuts on* OLIVER, *she gets up and picks up the red engagement book that has fallen to the floor. Straighten-*

ing herself after stooping.) What am I doing here—with *fifteen* of them! (*As* BENT *looks a bit taken aback.*) *Minutes!—Unique!—Fifteen!* What are they *for!*

BENT. Not for resting. (*Coming near her.*) There's a bit of life coming.

SHE. Yes. I know. (*Suddenly aware* BENT *shouldn't be there.*) I thought you were *out.*

BENT. (*Sour.*) She gave me the slip. (*Sour-meditative.*) To hell with women, m'lady. I'm fed up. (*Picks up her tray.*)

SHE. (*Rising, intent on herself.*) And *I'm fed up!* (*Paces away—turning round.*) Or shall I say it nobly?— I want to change my life—absolutely! Suddenly, publicly —so that it *can't* be taken back!

BENT. I should think twice.

SHE. I want to get *out!* (*Picking up and shaking the engagement book.*) *Out* of this book—with its procession —moving me on!—*Out* of the theatre! What am I doing playing these—fabricated—women!—Running north, south, east, west—inside a playwright's brain!

BENT. There's many'd give their eyes to do it.

SHE. (*Moving Downstage.*) In the spring it's my seventieth birthday. Like a Roll-Call. "Stand up," saith the Lord, "and call your number! Your time's up!"—Thus saith the Lord. (*Completely to* BENT—*but not aware of it.*) And then He takes me—at my weakest corner. Breaks me—where some screw or bolt's not doing its job. I shall be laid suddenly on a bed that I despise! Not my own bed. Not chosen by me. But the last bed. Dragged off into the Infinite, as it were, from a pub.—Like the one with curtains on the doors—where you fetch sandwiches.

BENT. (*Eyes shining—after all, what an audience he is!*) That'd make 'em sit up!

SHE. (*Echoing—bemused.*) "Sit up." . . .

BENT. Among the Curtain Calls!

SHE. (*Still half there and half not.*) Tonight?

BENT. Pub and all—just as you said it!

SHE. (*Sharp—alert.*) *How long have I got?*

BENT. (*Pulling the turnip watch out on its chain and holding it for her to see.*) I can't see it.

SHE. (*Stooping a little to see it.*) Ten minutes. (*He picks up tray and goes to kitchen door.*) I could say it— lightly . . .

BENT. (*Turning in surprise.*) Eh?

SHE. (*To herself.*) . . . almost as a joke. I'm so afraid of a grandiose ending. (*Pause.*) And after all, it's a wild thing to do!—Put down that tray.—I mean one could suggest—without making it certain. Tell Mr. Oliver. . . . He said he wasn't coming. But tell him—*most particularly.* . . . Say it like that! Say that I *beg* him to come tonight. Give me—still—ten minutes. . . . I want to try and remember . . . what I said just now. . . . (BENT *goes over to the door to go out. Coming downstairs in the half darkness, trying out her voice.*) Ladies and Gentlemen . . . (*Clears her throat.*) old friends of so many years . . . (*Haltingly.* BENT, *fascinated, lingers.*) when one puts things in one's own words . . .

BENT. (*Low—sly.*) . . . and no author to help you . . .

SHE. (*Appearing to take no notice—but made firm by opposition.*) Ladies and Gentlemen . . . old friends . . . I have come to a decision. In the Spring it's my seventieth birthday. Like a Roll-Call. "Stand up," said the Lord, "and call your number!" (CURTAIN *begins—either here or a little earlier—to come down as she says:*) "Your time's up! . . . but the lucky ones have a margin. . . ."

CURTAIN

ACT ONE

SCENE 2

Some months later. Very early Spring. In fact, The Birthday. Before luncheon. The room is much the same. The sofa has either gone or is in the background. In

*the foreground is the armchair; and a small table of
wrapped-up presents. Plates, glasses, etc. are on the
console table.*

BENT *is discovered sitting on the sofa, a cheap paper bag
beside him. A pink and white iced birthday cake is
on the low table. He is rapidly sticking birthday candles into the icing of the cake. When he has got in
half a dozen he pulls out a fresh bundle—realizes the
size of his task, reverses gear on the undertaking,
throws the bundle back in the bag and pulls out the
six candles, and as* SHE *comes in from her bedroom,
he rapidly shuts up the bag and hides it. Rises—
presents candle-less cake to her.*

SHE. (*With distaste.*) Seventy!

BENT. Well, you knew you would be.

SHE. What!

BENT. One sees it coming.

SHE. You've been so surly since I left the theatre!

BENT. (*A grumble.*) Why did you?

SHE. It was an act of folly! What have I gained by it!
Seventy was a mountain I wanted to survey! To make an
exploration! But I've been a woman in public so long—
this gift to myself befogs me!

BENT. *Gift* to yourself?

SHE. Of a private life. I don't know how to lead it!—
Without the theatre I feel diminished. Caught in so small
a programme! I put on clothes. I take them off. Eat.
Sleep. And in between . . . No sense of God!

BENT. Had you expected one?

SHE. One would have thought—some brush of a
wing. . . . He might have winked. (*Pause.*) The engagement book is there just the same—but the appointments
are meaner! (*To the window.*) Nobody here! How late
they are! It's only the Old who are punctual! I'm more
vulnerable to petty things! Your mind on your wife—the
house not running—fewer flowers!

(OLIVER *comes in in a hurry with flowers.*)

OLIVER. I'm late— Oh God, one's always kept by something. . . . *Happy* Birthday! (*Glancing around.*) Hell, I forgot the cake! Who ordered it?

BENT. Her Ladyship remembered. *She* ordered it.

OLIVER. No candles?

BENT. *I* remembered. But I decided against them.— Sooner or later one's got to stop counting. (*Goes.*)

SHE. I hate that trick! He gets it out of plays!

BENT. What?

SHE. Those postscripts at the door. Is Roxane coming?

OLIVER. I reminded her. (*Avoiding.*) Open your presents. (*Stooping.*) That's her writing!—Open it!

SHE. (*Taking the parcel, weighing it in her hand. Handing it back.*) I'm afraid to. (*He takes it.*) I asked you.—*Is* she coming?

OLIVER. (*Reluctantly.*) She stayed last night with a friend.

SHE. Is *that* your married life? (*Waits.*) Having your own house has made no difference?

OLIVER. It's made this difference—that I've started to write again. (*With surprise.*) It's a bottle of gin!—Why should she send you that!

SHE. She knows I like my tipple.

OLIVER. How much do you drink?

SHE. Too much for me.

OLIVER. For your health?

SHE. I shall take a lot of killing.

OLIVER. When did you begin?

SHE. Don't talk about beginning! It's a respectable habit—that grows less respectable with time!

OLIVER. But when?

SHE. When I needed mystery at sunset. When the cards grew dim.—*She* came in—your wife—it was the day you left here—and I obscured the bottle.—It wasn't what I had drunk that caught her fancy!—It was the gesture!

OLIVER. She is jealous of you. She says it isn't fair that you are past the age of beauty—and still in it.

SHE. (*Delighted.*) It was always a trick I played on

people! I was never beautiful.—I invented it! Does she know how beautiful *she* is?

OLIVER. She can never be sure of it. I watch her as she dresses and undresses feverishly in front of the mirror. It's painful!—I love her.—Every dress she wears—*ravishes* me!

SHE. Do you know that I feel guilty?

OLIVER. For what?

SHE. I have made you defenseless against her. I have made you so specially a woman's son.—In a way—you hardly had a father!

OLIVER. Biologically difficult!

SHE. Psychologically easy!—Roxane—*jealous* of me! Is it because she has married the son of my heart?

OLIVER. She was afraid of you—and she doesn't forgive it. She said when I brought her to you that she was frightened of a woman with sons.

SHE. I was willing—in theory—to have them taken from me. I was prepared to open my narrow charmed circle. But it took me by surprise to have the circle broken!

OLIVER. She said you were on the lookout for bandits!

SHE. No, I could have stood a bandit.

(BENT *comes in with the midday papers.*)

OLIVER. You've got a bandit in the other one!

SHE. (*Sharp.*) *Alice!* What's Alice been doing?

OLIVER. I was going to tell you. It's in the midday papers—

BENT. It's *headlines!*

OLIVER. Shop-lifting.

SHE. *Shop-lifting!*—Alice! (*To* OLIVER.) What's Tarver doing?

OLIVER. He won't do anything. I've just stood bail for her.

SHE. Why you? Why not Tarver?

OLIVER. (*Rueful.*) Because you have decreed I am the tender one!

SHE. (*As* BENT *brings her the newspaper.*) What shop was it?

BENT. Fortnums. (*Exits.*)

SHE. (*To* OLIVER.) Ring Cazan. The solicitor. He gets everyone out of scrapes. No—wait. He was buried yesterday. . . . That's why I thought of him! Who do I know who could help? Don't *you* know anyone?

OLIVER. Take my advice. Don't pull strings. Today everyone relies so on something else—that everyone forgets everything.

SHE. Is she alone? Where is she?

OLIVER. I offered to drive her home. Home—or anywhere. She went into a pub.

SHE. Why didn't you go after her?

OLIVER. By the look she gave me she would have bitten me.

TARVER. (*In doorway—grim.*) Happy Birthday.

SHE. (*Turning.*) No—a shocking one!—Why didn't *you* go bail for her?

TARVER. I'm finished with Alice!—I'm for my career.

SHE. Have you thought what's to become of her?

TARVER. She's been headed downhill ever since I married her.

SHE. Is it your fault?

TARVER. (*Crossing to her.*) Who knows? (*Stoops and kisses her.*) Who knows when the evil starts? When I married her, I suppose I married all that's behind her.

SHE. Nonsense! You and Alice are responsible together for her vices! Why does everyone blame the ancestors? Before I can turn round the failure of both your marriages will be on *my* shoulders!

OLIVER. Mine hasn't failed yet. (*To* TARVER.) Had you a row?

TARVER. One of many.—She asked me for money.

SHE. Why didn't you give it to her?

TARVER. She has enough.

SHE. Enough for what?

TARVER. To run our lives together.

SHE. She must have wanted more for her own life.

TARVER. Are you against me?

SHE. How should I know! You exclude me from knowing.

OLIVER. (*Turning the point of pain. Smiling.*) He preserves you from crossing his married frontier!

TARVER. Well, of course! Because you'd say you had heard it all before.

OLIVER. (*Lightly.*) And the battles of a man and his wife should be as fresh as dew! (*To his* MOTHER.) Does Tarver hurt you?

SHE. (*Absently—she has been pursuing her own thought.*) I've been thinking—if Tarver is half my immortality I shall have to rely more on Oliver. (*Suddenly coming-to.*) Yes, Tarver hurts me. I *so* hate blame! At my age the charming thing would be to be above criticism! (*To* TARVER—*direct.*) Remember! She's still your wife.

TARVER. Until I can get rid of her.

ALICE. (*In doorway.*) That'll be difficult. (*She walks unsteadily. She is followed into the room by an enormous man with a flaming head of red hair.*) Hullo, Oliver.

(ALICE *has a new rebel-surface. She wears whatever is the anti-uniform when this play is finally produced.*)

MAN. Are you all right now, madam?

ALICE. No. Stay with me.

MAN. (*To* OLIVER.) She wasn't well.

ALICE. I was sick in the pub. I owe him the taxi, too. Could you settle it, Tarver?—No. Better, Oliver. He's easier with the purse. (*To* MAN.) Wait a minute. Sit down. . . . Mama . . . can he have a drink?

SHE. Of course. Why don't we open the champagne now?

ALICE. I see you've got gin there. (*Picks up bottle.*) It's quicker to open. (*Sees card attached.*) From Roxy!— Funny present! (*Strips off the lead cover round the top. Offers bottle to* MAN.) Help yourself. Glasses over there.

MAN. I don't drink. Which is your husband?

ALICE. Him.

MAN. (*To* TARVER.) She's in trouble. You ought to look after her.

TARVER. Mind your own business.

MAN. She *is* my business. I brought her here.

TARVER. D'you want me to punch your nose for you?

MAN. You'd get nowhere. This is a straight girl in straight trouble. I'm watching to see how you treat her.

TARVER. (*To* ALICE.) How fast you make friends!

ALICE. He's religious.

TARVER. Does that explain it?

ALICE. He does a good deed every day.

MAN. (*Showing a huge doubled fist. Calm.*) I don't find it difficult with this behind it.

TARVER. You're nothing but a bully.

MAN. (*Calm.*) Say that again.

TARVER. No. I prefer once only.

MAN. (*To* ALICE.) Shall I take you out of here?

SHE. (*To* MAN—*suddenly.*) And where would you take her? (*Looks at him—waiting.*) She's got her own home. And her husband's here to take her there.

MAN. That's up to her.

SHE. No, it's up to *me*. This is my house and these are my relations. You can't punch me at my age. So it's safe for me to talk to you! I don't like people as simple as you are! It's no good hammering life into black and white because you've got a fist like a sirloin!

ALICE. (*In laughter.*) Oh, I do like Mama! Oh, God, I like Mama when she gets going!

SHE. (*Gathering momentum.*) And what's more—you are complicating life for me! I don't like strangers taking sides! There are enough sides taken with my own children! I don't like brute force simply walking into my drawing room! I don't like Boy Scouts when they are as big as you are! Accept the money for the taxi and please go.

ALICE. (*Her hand on the* MAN's *arm.*) Go along. You've had it! Our romance is over!

MAN. (*As* OLIVER *comes up to him with a "paying for*

taxi" face and gesture.) Keep your half crowns. I've got a yacht and a Bentley.

ALICE. You've got a . . . *What* have I let slip through my fingers!

MAN. Red Gus Risko.

ALICE. The one on the placards outside the Albert Hall! The *Boxer!* Oh, I ought to have known! Why didn't you tell me!

MAN. Because I like to do my good deeds quietly. (*He goes out, followed by* OLIVER.)

ALICE. (*To* TARVER.) So you were talking of getting rid of me.

TARVER. I'll speak to you when you're sober.

ALICE. I'm not drunk. I had a glass of beer and it made me sick, owing to emotion. I'm faint now. I could eat . . . (*Seeing the birthday cake.*) Oh! . . . Mama! Of *course!* It's your birthday!

SHE. Cut it and eat it. (*Crossly.*) *I* had to remember to buy it.

ALICE. No, *you* must cut it! (*Carries cake and knife to her. To* TARVER.) You can't get rid of me—unless I'm mad or unfaithful. And even then it's legally difficult. I'm going to remain your wife and damage your career.

TARVER. Well, you've done it.

ALICE. (*Taking a piece of cake.*) Not sufficiently.

TARVER. What lies did you tell that creature?

ALICE. I said you kept me short of money and you beat me. He's very chivalrous and gets inflamed very quickly. But Mama's right. He's too simple.

TARVER. So when you took the bag in the shop it was aimed at me?

ALICE. (*Mouth full of cake.*) That's right.

TARVER. (*To his* MOTHER.) I'm glad you hear it.

SHE. I had no idea that you beat her.

TARVER. Nor I, either! It must be nearly luncheon time.

SHE. (*Swiftly.*) I had expected you to lunch here!

TARVER. You never said we were to come!

SHE. Yes, I did. I asked all four. Formally. By letter.

ALICE. I never got any letter.

TARVER. Nor I. . . .

SHE. (*To* TARVER.) Couldn't you dine tonight?

TARVER. I am dining with a client.

SHE. Put him off. The birthday of a woman who is old and famous . . . is sad and important. Alice? Or shall you be in prison?

ALICE. I'm out on bail. I don't think the law works as fast as that.

SHE. (*Suddenly seeing the letters.*) *Gracious!* . . . *Here they all are!—stamped.* And never posted! (*Puts her finger on a bunch of envelopes.*) You see what it is— Bent is so old! He's totally forgotten them! Well—stay all the same. We can picnic in here.

ALICE. And Roxy?

SHE. Roxane's not coming. (*To* TARVER.) Where's Oliver? Go and fetch Oliver. (*Directly he goes out. To* ALICE *—with urgency.*) Is your marriage worth mending?

ALICE. He doesn't try to understand me!

SHE. He knows by instinct that he mustn't!—Quick! Is it worth mending?

ALICE. I can't . . . all in a minute . . . I shouldn't think so. I don't know. What's the real heart of him? What's his breaking point? Can I win by fighting? What's he made of?

SHE. I don't know, either.

ALICE. But you . . . you . . .

SHE. Yes, but they change so. I'm afraid of him. The baby isn't the boy and the boy isn't the man and when he's old there'll be no link, either.

ALICE. Did you say—afraid of him?

SHE. Out of my reach then! He has something implacable and male that's grown. . . . Hush.

(BOTH MEN *come back.*)

OLIVER. Tarver says he won't stay if Alice is staying.

(TARVER, *side-tracking by the writing table, looks down onto it.*)

ALICE. Tarver can't eat while he's hating.

SHE. Nonsense!

TARVER. (*To his* MOTHER.) They're *not* addressed to us! (*Picks one up.*) They're bills you're paying! You've invented those invitations! Why?—Is the food a myth, too?

SHE. (*Dignified.*) There is champagne. And the cake there.

TARVER. You *can't* ride out on that! . . . (*Enter* BENT, *carrying a small tray delicately laid for one, probably a vegetable and egg salad in a pretty bowl, perhaps sticks of celery in a glass, obviously for one person.*) What's that?

BENT. Her Ladyship's luncheon.

SHE. You know very well I told you to arrange for four! In the dining room!

BENT. No, you didn't.

(*As* SHE *puts her hand over her eyes.*)

OLIVER. What's the matter?

SHE. I don't feel well. I feel giddy. (*Sits down: eyes closed. Waving her hand at the tray.*) Take that food out of my sight! (*He puts the tray down on the side.*) If I sit quietly here . . .

OLIVER. Get her champagne, Tarver!

SHE. (*Faintly.*) Didn't Alice say—gin acts quicker? (*Fans her face with a newspaper.*) Give me—Roxane's . . . horrible present. . . .

OLIVER. (*To* BENT.) How often has my mother had an attack like this?

BENT. Hardly . . . (*Stuck between two loyalties.*) ever.

ALICE. (*Smiling—low.*) In fact never.

BENT. (*To nobody.*) But on one's seventieth birthday —why shouldn't something begin? I mean—we've got to get the door open, haven't we? *Something's* got to start coming undone. . . .

SHE. (*Annoyed—to* BENT.) Nonsense! Every thread

and stitch and lock and hook of my life's in place—whatever simile you are using! (*As he picks up the tray.*) Leave that there! I may want it later.

(BENT *goes.*)

TARVER. (*Waiting till he has gone.*) What was all that about lunch, Mother?

SHE. It was an impulse!—Use your imagination! . . . I wanted to see if you would stay! I *wanted* you to stay! For that matter I wanted you to want to *come!*—You all send me flowers but . . . What I wanted was for you yourselves to be here!

TARVER. Well, we are!

SHE. But only for a morning visit. I wanted you all to want that . . . little festivity of a meal. *Together.* As we used to have it.

TARVER. Why didn't you ask us?

SHE. I thought *you* would have done the asking. And —when you didn't . . . I didn't, either! And when you came I wanted to see if . . . to know if . . . (*A little break in her voice.*) when I asked—you'd *accept!*

TARVER. Well, I didn't! (*Pause.*) And now you get a son back.

SHE. What do you mean?

TARVER. You said you saw me oftener before I married. Now I'm going to be *un*married.

SHE. (*In a wail.*) It won't be the same! You've outgrown me! You will be looking for women and it will be all to do over again! The love and the disappointment and the unadjustability! And the sense of silence and the things you think I shouldn't say!—And the false sweetness to the new woman! And her disapproval of me. I hate disapproval more than anything! I should like to be a miracle—as I used to be! (*To* OLIVER—*a quiver in her voice.*) You must find me the Chinese Prime Minister!

OLIVER. Tar—it's her birthday.

SHE. You think I'm going to cry? Well, it may be. The

dearest thing in the world to me is my vanity. (*To* TAR-
VER—*who is on the point of going.*) Aren't you going to
drink my health!—*Do* stay! I want to talk of *me!*

ALICE. Tarver's right. We can't be nice to you on a private volcano.—*I'll* go. (*Moves to near door.*)

SHE. No! I want you more than anyone! You're such
a woman!

(TARVER *picks up his document bag.*)

ALICE. "Such a woman"?

SHE. Violent, and selfish. And desperate to live for herself. It's a relief to have someone here—like me.

ALICE. Like you? But I've no fame in front of me—

TARVER. Must you have your eyes always on yourself?

ALICE. Always—always on myself! Like all of us here!
—Except Oliver. All of us wanting to leave some mark!
Even Mama. . . .

SHE. Most of all Mama—God help her! (*To* ALICE.)
I see no hope for you with Tarver! Stay—as a young
woman stranger. Who is going to have another life!

ALICE. Ten to one I'm going to prison—if that's a life.

SHE. When I was a girl . . . I *wanted* to go to prison!
(TARVER *smiles at her.*) Well, all right. I wasn't always
a mother! Nor even chiefly a mother! You seem to forget! I was what they call spirited. I thought then that no
harm could come to me that I couldn't turn into a triumph.—*What are you thinking of, Oliver!*

OLIVER. Roxane.

SHE. No wonder I prefer Alice to be here and Roxane
not! Daughters-in-law unloved by their husbands are my
cup of tea!

OLIVER. The expression is unlike you!

SHE. I thought of grist to the mill and discarded it. I
find I don't lay my hands on words as nimbly as I used
to do. Open the champagne, Tarver! I am seventy—I am
famous—I am your mother.—Talk about me as in an
obituary! How do you consider me? It seems a pity that
for once . . . Or am I maudlin?

ALICE. (*Thoughtfully.*) I don't believe we *can* consider you . . . until you're gone.

SHE. (*Note of panic.*) So while I live I shall *never* know what you think!

TARVER. (*To* ALICE.) There's no need to be so frank that you're cruel!

ALICE. I thought Mama and I were on a very high wind of truth.

BENT. (*To nobody in particular.*) The wind was too high for her.

SHE. (*Disregarding—to* ALICE.) So to you—what I *am* doesn't matter?

ALICE. Yes, it does.

SHE. But not what I have *been?*

ALICE. I suppose you can become history. But you can't make us *feel* what you have been.

BENT. It's blowing gales.

SHE. Where are you going, Oliver?

OLIVER. I think I shall ring her.

SHE. In my bedroom? Well, ring her. You look vacant.

OLIVER. No. I won't ring her.

SHE. Oh, I hate vacillation! Is Roxane to stand in the wings—I have a sense of being understudied till I am nearly off the stage. I want to speak about the Past'—which Alice says is gone. I want to tell you both about your father—

OLIVER. (*Lightly—he is on the whole bored.*) *What* about him?

SHE. (*Lamely.*) He left me.

OLIVER. Well, of course.

SHE. Why "of course"?

OLIVER. Of course we know.

SHE. It came out in a curious manner!

OLIVER. Was it for another woman?

SHE. No! He adored me!

OLIVER. (*Lightly.*) Then were *you* in the wrong!

BENT. Don't egg her on, Mr. Oliver. Ask for the Past . . .

SHE. *Leave the room!*

BENT. and you never know what you'll get. . . .

SHE. . . . *this minute. (He goes. Immediately—to* OLIVER.) What did you mean?

OLIVER. (*Smiling.*) One can't ask one's mother if she had lovers!

SHE. D'you think I've forgotten!

TARVER. I hope you can't remember!

SHE. Why that tone?

TARVER. Respect.

SHE. Can't I get *out* of being a parent? Can't you listen to a woman!—Does love change?—And jealousy?—And torment—and possession? The *power*—the *fall* from power!—The reverse situation!—A whole landscape of love about which I am talking!

OLIVER. (*Completely undercutting, intent on his own love. Nearing bedroom door.*) If I don't ring her now I may miss her. . . .

SHE. *Oliver!*

OLIVER. (*Disappears into bedroom.*) I won't be two minutes. . . .

SHE. (*Rising and crossing swiftly to the bedroom door.*) Can one shout the Past after a train in motion?

OLIVER. (*Reappearing in doorway.*) What's the matter!

SHE. I feel embalmed!—Like a bishop in stone—or those kneeling women like vases—with seventeen children! Yes—Oliver, yes! You were embarrassed to ask—*Yes!*—I had lovers!

OLIVER. I don't believe it.

SHE. Do you find it incredible?

OLIVER. No. Not incredible. I hear you say it.

SHE. Well?

OLIVER. Well, I must examine . . .

SHE. What?

OLIVER. Whose son I am.

SHE. Your *father's!*

OLIVER. Of course. But which?

SHE. That's *not* what I meant!

OLIVER. You said it. So I am illegitimate. It might ac-

count for my nature and its complications. . . . And
your domination of me. And my inability to master her!

SHE. Stop, Oliver!

OLIVER. And why I had to be the tender one.—And
for *whom!* (*Bitterly.*) I'm the one who is so aware of
the heart I can't move in any direction! (*Postscript
thought.*) I think I shall take orders.

SHE. From whom?

OLIVER. (*Savagely.*) Holy Orders.—I'm going home.

SHE. Wait! I'm prepared . . . D'you want the truth!
Can you bear the truth . . . Oh, for God's sake, I'm not
in the dock! Must I call across the room!—I told you I
was unfaithful to your father. I had no idea he was a
good man!

OLIVER. Why?

SHE. I had never met one. (*Invention flowing better
now.*) I had lived on my wits since I was fifteen.

TARVER. Your wits!

SHE. Would you rather I had lived on my appearance!
(*Pause.*) I did that, too. (*To* OLIVER—*quickly.*) Oh—
long before you were born! I ran away from home—I
was as pretty as Sin! (*With satisfaction.*) As pretty and
evil as an adder! I had nowhere to live—I'd have gone
on the streets—but . . . (*Pause.*) I was *rescued* by your
father!

TARVER. I seem to have heard . . .

SHE. What?

TARVER. . . . that line before. . . . (*Searching mem-
ory.*) Mrs. Warren's Profession!

SHE. (*Quick.*) Why not! *I knew the author!*

TARVER. (*Smiling.*) Is that—accurate?

SHE. How can the Past be accurate—on demand! As
though it was the gas bill! I was the rage in Bloomsbury!
I knew *all* the authors! They sat at my feet—singers and
poets and actors—here in this room! I remember . . .
(*Pause.*) six brothers. . . . (*Recollectory pause.*) Six—
identical—brothers.

ALICE. (*Fascinated.*) Why *identical?*

SHE. They all had the same reactions to me. Instantaneous, unmistakable!—And then—that other—*unrefusable* man! It was with him your father caught me! (*She begins to laugh.*) It was in this chair—with the mended leg. Your father broke it! Bent was just bringing in coffee. . . .

OLIVER. Don't laugh like that!

SHE. I *do* laugh like that! I'm laughing at my seventieth birthday!

OLIVER. *Stop!*

TARVER. Go *on.* We may never hear this again.

OLIVER. I don't want to hear it!

SHE. Nor ever asked for it—oh, this absorbed generation!

OLIVER. There's something *wrong!* About *all* of it!

SHE. (*Pious.*) Of course it was wrong.

OLIVER. I mean the *way* you tell it!—The way you *warm* to it!

ALICE. (*Slyly inserting her words like velvet.*) But all the same—you see—she has got your attention.

SHE. *You* don't believe me?

ALICE. No.

SHE. Was I so absurd then?

ALICE. I took your Past away. You are putting it back again.

SHE. And if I tell you truth or lies—isn't it the need that tells them?—I *meant* to be absurd! I wanted to bring home to you—that nobody ever asks!—And I *need* to be alive—as I was then—and *am! Now*—as much as ever! (*Picking up her glass.*) To Alice's rebellion—which was also mine!

ALICE. You felt that too—in your time. . . .

SHE. (*Indignant.*) "In my time"! . . . The thing's a ribbon—not a set of beads. It's joined—it flows. What is this egotism called "Modern" which, like the hymns, becomes "Ancient" before you can turn round! What you feel—I felt. And so did the Greeks. And so they will in the moon! But I shall be gone—and there'll be no trace of me! I shall be ashes—and you won't admit that there were embers.—And I care—I *care*—not what you think of me—but that you should know what *kind* of woman I was!—Go! All of you!—I want my *own* Contemporary! The man to whom I mattered! Who knew . . . who knows . . . (*Absolute change of tone to the practical.*) *Bent!* Ring *Sir Gregory!*

(*They are frozen.*)

BENT. There you are, you see!

OLIVER. My . . . father . . .

SHE. The Savoy. Temple Bar 4343.

BENT. (*As he dials.*) All the dead are at the Savoy.

SHE. Extension 217.

TARVER. *This* is hysteria!

SHE. It is *not*. I am only *frantic*.

OLIVER. You can't bring back the dead, Mother.

MRS. FOREST. (*Crossing the stage to the telephone— takes it from* BENT.) Gregory! Are you alive? (*Follows the longest pause ever made in the theatre. She listens— with changing expressions.*) I relent. Eight o'clock. To- night. (*Pause. As she walks to her bedroom door.*) If his being dead is the biggest lie of all . . . (*Arrives at door.*) and I prove it true . . . (*Just before door shuts.*) we have a ghost for dinner.

CURTAIN

ACT TWO

Before dinner the same evening.

BENT *is in full evening butler's rig. Though married, he still no doubt keeps some clothes at the house.*

BENT. (*Mutinous—insisting.*) But there's the dining room, m'lady!

SHE. (*In an evening dress of splendour.*) We can't have dinner in there. The fire smokes. There's a bird's nest in the chimney.

BENT. But it's a warm spring evening.

SHE. There should always be a fire burning. It makes the silver flicker. Do as I say . . . (*Suddenly encountering a more obstinate look.*) and pull yourself together!— Or I shall telephone to *Mrs.* Bent to come round and help me.

BENT. (*Trembling with instant rage.*) That young woman doesn't put her nose in here!

SHE. You should never have married so young a woman. It always brings a loss of dignity.

BENT. (*Muttering.*) There's other things to marriage.

SHE. Don't make me blush for you.

BENT. With that dress, m'lady, it *should* be the dining room.

SHE. (*Flat.*) It's a fork supper.

BENT. (*Disgusted.*) What am I here for, then!

SHE. To hand plates out and take them back again. Odd jobs and no ritual.

BENT. (*Etherealised.*) I don't exist, m'lady, without ritual. I'm an empty coat—hanging on a line.

SHE. Ah, Bent—your preoccupation with images!

BENT. Snatches of 'em—snatches of 'em come back, Madam.

SHE. Why—"Madam"?

BENT. I was thinking back, far back, to when you were

35

Madam. To when you first engaged me—I came to you to study life. I had literary aspirations. I should have written a book.

SHE. (*Absently.*) What would it have been about?

BENT. Upper class life. But the life vanished. (*Ferociously and suddenly.*) And *sex.*

SHE. (*Startled.*) Sex . . .

BENT. (*Still fierce.*) It's a big deterrent! It's brought me to battle with unworthy women!

SHE. (*Glancing at herself across the room into a mirror.*) How do I look?

BENT. (*Mechanically.*) No different.

SHE. (*Turning round in surprise.*) Nonsense!

BENT. To tell you the truth, I can't see.

SHE. (*Sitting down.*) Nor can I. It was charming of God! I never expected it! . . .

BENT. Eh?

SHE. (*Glancing again at the mirror from where she sits.*) . . . That as beauty vanishes the eyes grow dimmer. I look in the glass and the outline seems as good as ever! In the illusory haze . . . (*Sits bolt upright moving her head to loosen it on the shoulders.*) . . . I make for mystery! (*Breaking off.*) But one must keep the spine straight! (*Stretching her neck and feeling the neck muscles with one hand.*) There's the hall door!

BENT. (*Going slowly to the door. Turning with his hand on the handle.*) Are the young gentlemen of an age for love?

SHE. (*Impatient.*) How you forget! They're married! . . .

(*The door opens.* TARVER *has let himself in.*)

TARVER. (*Impeccably dressed—black tie. Coming in quickly—urgent.*) Mother . . .

SHE. (*Stately—dignified.*) It was good of you to come.

TARVER. (*Impatient.*) Naturally I came! Before they come—and it's why I've come early . . .

SHE. I don't want to answer questions to you alone!

TARVER. I must know where I stand! (*Going near street window—evidently anxious to get something out before the others come.*) I'm the elder! How long have you been in touch with . . . this man?

SHE. "This man"! I won't answer!

TARVER. (*Extreme annoyance—looking out of window.*) It's Alice! Good God. . . . That creature! He's brought her in his Bentley! (*Turning back from window.*) You must forbid her!

SHE. What?

TARVER. Oh, good heavens, you must see that if it's my father . . . Is *he* to be in the room?

(*The door opens.* ALICE *comes in. The* BOXER, *being nervous, keeps out of sight behind her for a moment.*)

SHE. (*Outraged—to* ALICE.) You've not *changed!*

ALICE. (*Rebellious retention of ego.*) No. This is how I *am.*

SHE. (*Now aware of* BOXER *in doorway, carrying box.*) Good God—*again?*

ALICE. He's brought you foie gras.

TARVER. (*Furious—to* ALICE.) This is *too* much!

ALICE. (*Wilfully getting him wrong.*) Much too much! It cost him twenty pounds. I *dote* on extravagance!

SHE. So do I—more plates, however.—Tell him to come in but warn him not to use his hands. (OLIVER *appears, properly dressed. Sharp.*) Where's Roxane ?

OLIVER. She hasn't come back.

SHE. Thank God for that! I want *all* Oliver here!—And not half!

OLIVER. All of me *is* here!—I want to speak to . . . Sir Gregory—with a clear mind.

TARVER. (*To* ALICE—*angrily.*) It's monstrous of you to have brought that man!—And *frivolous!*

ALICE. You'll find a stranger a help in what's coming.

TARVER. What's coming?

ALICE. Awkwardness.

TARVER. (*Sharp.*) Bent!—The bell!

BENT. Yes, Sir Gregory.

TARVER. (*As* BENT *goes to the door.*) Don't you know who I am!

BENT. (*At door.*) Not just at the moment. (*Goes out.*)

TARVER. (*In the apprehensive silence. To* OLIVER.) Are you prepared!

OLIVER. (*Grimly.*) For *anyone.*

ALICE. (*Mocking—to her* MOTHER-IN-LAW.) Who have you persuaded . . . (*Cocking an ear at the door.*) into taking off his coat out there!

SHE. (*Smiling.*) Still not convinced!

BENT. (*Scared—returning, holding door shut against someone behind him.*) It's Sir Gregory's . . . father, m'lady. . . . (*Fumbling with relationships.*) It's your ladyship's . . . father-in-law. . . .

SIR GREGORY. (*A very personable strong old man. Nearly pushing* BENT *down as he bursts door open.*) I should need to be a hundred and twenty, you silly ass, to be her father-in-law! (*Half crossing room.*) My wife! At *last!*

BENT. (*Recovering his balance—mumbling.*) I remember that voice . . . "you silly ass." . . .

OLIVER. (*Urgent—suspicious.*) But do you remember *him?*

BENT. I remember the night he went . . .

(SIR GREGORY *stops dead.*)

SHE. (*Imperious.*) Bent—go and sit in my bedroom!

BENT. Is there a bell?

SIR GREGORY. (*Shouting at him.*) No, there isn't! Just *go!*

TARVER. (*Suspicious.*) How did you know?

SIR GREGORY. Because I pulled the bell out of the wall a long time ago!—Do you doubt it?

OLIVER. *I* do.

SIR GREGORY. (*Over his shoulder as he goes to his* WIFE.) Who are you?

OLIVER. Another . . . son.

SIR GREGORY. Impregnable woman! It's been a siege! (*Taking her hand.*) You haven't changed!

SHE. The only man to whom I seem young!

SIR GREGORY. The only man in the world who *knows* you are young!—I have remembered your birthday—but I haven't remembered your age!

SHE. What can happen to me after seventy?

SIR GREGORY. *I* have happened to you! Do you remember?

SHE. (*Smiling.*) No!

SIR GREGORY. (*Gay.*) But I remember!—And, oh, she was a handful!

SHE. *That's* what I wanted to hear!

SIR GREGORY. *And* Lausanne! *And* Paris!—*and* Roumania!—And the row in the canal! At Emms!—I've brought you diamonds. (*Snaps it open.* ALICE *pushes up to see.*) Who are you?

ALICE. (*On guard.*) Don't you know?

SIR GREGORY. Yes, I do!—Shocking!—Your face was in the newspapers. (*To his* WIFE.) How beautifully you touch jewels! (*Glances at* ALICE.) But keep them away from the Shop-Lifter!

ALICE. Are you rich?

SIR GREGORY. Very rich.

ALICE. How rich?

SIR GREGORY. I am Advisor to the Sheik of Mwelta. I guard his interests while he prays by his oil wells. I see they don't chisel him out of his royalties. We are all rich there but the Sheik and I are the richest. Keep it dark. But in the family I let you know.

ALICE. Do you come often to London?

SIR GREGORY. Last autumn was the first time in twenty-nine years.—I live in the Sheik's pocket! It's not safe to leave it. (*Pause.*) And when I *do* come—my wife won't see me!

SHE. That's how we arranged it.

OLIVER. Why couldn't you have come here—if it's your own house?

SIR GREGORY. That's my business! (*Cold-shouldering him. To his* WIFE.) Did you get the caviar?

SHE. I did indeed.

SIR GREGORY. (*Complacent.*) The best Beluga. Two jars.

SHE. I sent them back. (*At his look of surprise.*) How could I have explained them!

SIR GREGORY. In your own house you could have explained an octopus! (*Wrathfully—to* TARVER.) Do you bully her?

(SHE *begins to laugh.*)

TARVER. Certainly not!

SIR GREGORY. (*To* OLIVER.) And *you?*

OLIVER. (*Polite.*) Have you come back to the wrong wife—Sir?

TARVER. My brother means that perhaps you are not the right husband.

ALICE. (*As* SIR GREGORY *is about to explode on* TARVER. *Flattering him.*) You look so young for someone so long dead, Sir Gregory.

SIR GREGORY. (*Mollified.*) Then why did old Bent think I was a hundred and twenty!

SHE. He slipped up among the generations!

OLIVER. After twenty-nine years are you sure, Mother?

SHE. (*Lightly. Smiling up into* SIR GREGORY's *face.*) How can I be!

SIR GREGORY. (*Instantly—stooping.*) I haven't kissed you yet. . . .

SHE. (*Dodging the kiss—waving it away.*) Pay a little attention to your sons!

SIR GREGORY. I remember a little boy—touching and manly. . . . —*Tarver*—I gave you your name!

OLIVER. Do you remember *me?*

SHE. (*Introducing hurriedly.*) Oliver!

SIR GREGORY. I remember a baby. (*Pause.*) When I dine out and meet men—I don't necessarily feel tender towards them. I employ a great many men. I like a few. But not many.

OLIVER. Are you warning us?

SIR GREGORY. I am only saying that as I haven't watched either of you grow up, we are meeting on the level. I mean—neither side is weakened by affection. (*To* TARVER.) Are you in oil?

TARVER. The Middle Wells.

SIR GREGORY. How curious. The Sheik owns that one.

TARVER. Then—must I conclude—that it is through you—that I am where I am?

SIR GREGORY. I seem to remember making some such suggestion.

ALICE. (*Aside, to* TARVER.) Does that clinch it?

TARVER. (*Very short.*) Yes, it does. And I feel *enormously* irritated.

OLIVER. (*With cold sarcasm.*) What have you done for me, sir?

SIR GREGORY. Nothing.

OLIVER. Why do you discriminate between us?

SIR GREGORY. (*A half laugh.*) Some sort of natural vexation.

OLIVER. My mother says I am like you.

SIR GREGORY. (*They seem not to get on.*) I see nothing like you in me or like me in you.

OLIVER. I am struck by it!

SIR GREGORY. A man doesn't care for his sons to be too like him.—As with dogs—who *seem* so individual until you visit the breeders! (*Changing the subject.*) Who's the guest in the background?

ALICE. Another rich man.

SIR GREGORY. (*Delighted.*) But I *know* him! (*His hand out.*) I know who he is—at any rate! It's Red Gus Risko! (*To* BOXER.) You've got your Championship fight on your hands in four days! (*They shake hands.*) My God, I wish you well! Have you shed that last two pounds?

BOXER. There's four days still. And he's an easy touch! I'm not losing sleep over that left-hand artist! Things don't look too rosy for him!

SIR GREGORY. There's something about a heavyweight that's magic to me! You can have all your middle chaps and your little chaps. But a heavyweight fight is the most terrible breathless thing! Is it being televised?

BOXER. They won't allow it. May I send you ringside seats?

SIR GREGORY. I have to go back tomorrow to my Sheik.

OLIVER. This is unbearable! This—talk—from a man we thought dead! From a dead father!—I don't speak for Tarver but for me!—I'm *giddy!* I'm as giddy as if north and south were abolished! *Much* giddier! Look, Sir! Let's come to grips! In a single day—*today*—at the age of seventy—my mother reverses everything! She tells me she's not a widow—

SIR GREGORY. (*Chuckling.*) Nor she is!

OLIVER. —that she's not the mother we've known— that she's as evil as an adder—that you left her in disgust—that she behaved worse than Satan. . . .

SIR GREGORY. Women exaggerate, don't they?

OLIVER. That's no answer!

SIR GREGORY. She always told me lies! I loved 'em!

(*As they talk,* SHE *takes out a small vanity case, toys with it, opens and shuts it.*)

OLIVER. If nothing will move you—she tells us she had lovers!

SIR GREGORY. So she did!

SHE. Gregory—

SIR GREGORY. I threw one of them out of the house! That damn singer!

SHE. Get your father a drink, Tarver!

ALICE. (*As if it were to herself.*) It seems shocking, doesn't it, that one should be old . . . and yet have slept with someone?

SHE. It seems shocking . . . (*Deliberately lifts the open vanity case and contemplates her own face in it.*) that there should be no record of it!

SIR GREGORY. (*Looking at* OLIVER.) No *record!*

SHE. (*Hastily.*) That is *not* what I meant!

SIR GREGORY. If I hadn't promised—

OLIVER. Why are you glaring at me, Sir?

SIR GREGORY. But I never broke a promise in my life!

SHE. If you fight an old battle—where are the witnesses! And the evidence—obliterated!

SIR GREGORY. (*A glance at* OLIVER.) Not all of it. (*Suddenly inflamed.*) I could have the same blazing row now—

SHE. So could I!—You always insist on yes or no!

SIR GREGORY. Very normal.

SHE. No, it is *not* very normal! It doesn't take into account—the inner need! The urges of fantasy . . .

SIR GREGORY. (*To the* OTHERS.) Your mother's mind slides from the center to the periphery!

SHE. And with your *yes* and *no*—standing up like two lamp-posts—what about the invisible army behind them! The lies one tells oneself! The self-delusions! The lacks—for which one is compensating? The ache for conquest, the bragging, the ambition . . Whatever I said then—Yes—or *No*—had no meaning! You would *never* admit that there are two sides to a quarrel!

SIR GREGORY. It doesn't get you anywhere *to* admit it!

SHE. But to be got anywhere isn't what one's after! There's the delicate question of—what *happened!*

SIR GREGORY. Well, *what* happened?

SHE. What—here in this room?

SIR GREGORY. They are old enough to stand it!

SHE. (*Loftily.*) I remember only the *outlines* of the situations!

SIR GREGORY. (*Quite recovering.*) It isn't the wicked sides of women that inflame a man!—It's the nimble way they side-step when you blame 'em!

SHE. So you haven't changed! And you admit no faults. . . .

SIR GREGORY. Yes, I do. (*Picks up her hand. But she withdraws it.*) But I react fatally to contradiction! (*Seizes her roughly by the waist. Kisses her.*)

SHE. Oh . . . (*Touches her eyes with her handkerchief.*) That hasn't happened for . . .

SIR GREGORY. (*Sitting down beside her. Teasing and*

tender.) . . . how many years? (*To them* ALL.) Whatever have you been doing to her to bring all this about? Haven't you learnt how to treat her!

ALICE. I told her her Past was dead. . . .

SIR GREGORY. Don't you know she can't stand oblivion!

ALICE. (*Protecting herself*.) The Past she invented is dead—for none of it's true!

SIR GREGORY. What's true is that I worshipped her! She was the Burning Bush and the Apple of Eden and the silver snake on the Tree! (*Pause*.) And then all of a sudden she was like eczema to me!

SHE. What a horrible simile!

SIR GREGORY. Your mother-in-law is an exceptional and extraordinary woman!—She is outside rules!

ALICE. (*To* TARVER.) Would you come back to me—after half a lifetime—and say that to me, Tarver?

SIR GREGORY. (*To his* WIFE.) Don't they get on?

TARVER. We are fighting to the death, if you want to know. She defies me to get rid of her.

SIR GREGORY. Walk out of the house on her!

TARVER. But it's *my* house!

SIR GREGORY. What are a few possessions! You must be gentlemanly.—*I* left your mother. (*Chuckles*.) She never thought I would!

SHE. (*Murmuring*.) Hackles are rising.

SIR GREGORY. (*Patting her hand*.) The old yeast stirring . . . (*To* ALICE.) Why did you pinch the bag? Was it insanity?

ALICE. No. It was revenge.

SIR GREGORY. Revenge for what?

ALICE. His superiority.

SIR GREGORY. (*To* TARVER.) You simply can't keep 'em down unless you break them. It's no use—half measures. It only maddens them. They want to be right with a kind of passion. If you let them be right—well and good. But if you don't want them to be right you must half murder them.

ALICE. There speaks a husband!—I wish I'd married *you!*

SIR GREGORY. (*Meditatively—a reply at a tangent.*) What a horrible relationship.

TARVER. (*Taken aback.*) *Ours?*

SIR GREGORY. Marriage. The beginning and the end are wonderful. But the middle part is hell.

SHE. Shall we call Bent?

SIR GREGORY. (*With a smile.*) Side-stepping?

SHE. But he ought to be carving the turkey. (*To TARVER.*) Call Bent for me.

TARVER. (*Going to the bedroom door.*) Bent! . . . Bent! . . .

BENT. I'm coming! (*Stands, his hair a bit on end, in the doorway, supporting himself against the door jamb.*) I had a dream in there.

SHE. Carve the turkey.

BENT. I dreamt everything was still to come.

SHE. Carve the turkey.

BENT. Let me finish. There was ice on the pond in the village. She was the first girl I ever loved.—She was fourteen. (*He begins to skate.*)

SHE. (*Annoyed with herself.*) Oh! I'd *forgotten!*

TARVER. What?

SHE. I left it behind the looking glass. But he always found things!

BENT. (*Skating about the room as in his dream, his hands behind his back.*) She said she had tripped over a star. And when I looked she was right! The stars were in the ice, too!

SHE. Oh, Bent— Ah, Bent. Marvelously elliptical! Evocative!—The night ice and the girl!

SIR GREGORY. (*Muttering.*) Silly ass! Night-ice-nothing!

SHE. (*To TARVER.*) Carry him back to his dream again. Put him on my bed.—And *bring away the bottle.*

BENT. (*As TARVER comes up to him. Turning truculently to face him.*) Hands off, Sir Gregory! (*Moves back a pace and in doing so upsets a chair which falls backwards. Turning sharp, pointing to it—his old finger shaking.*) You know what happened. . . .

(*A burst of laughter from the real* SIR GREGORY.)

OLIVER. (*Quick.*) *What* happened?

(SHE *rises: warns* BENT *by a look to shut up.*)

BENT. (*Vague.*) There was a lot of love then about the house—
OLIVER. (*Sharp.*) How much of it did you see?
BENT. (*Still trying to keep it general.*) Cries behind doorways and arguments and high words and quarrels that burnt from room to room like marsh fires—
SHE. (*Very sharp.*) *Bent!*
BENT. (*Same technique.*) And she so taking and lively, with that shine of love like diamonds—
SHE. (*Furious and helpless.*) That's the *bottle!*
BENT. And the two of them fighting. Fisticuffs. Words of murder—
OLIVER. (*Cutting across this—to* SIR GREGORY.) *What* happened?
SIR GREGORY. I hit him.
OLIVER. What for?
SIR GREGORY. Something insufferable and not important.
BENT. (*Goaded.*) Not important! Me nearly throttled. And Her Ladyship flat on the floor!—You tried to get his name out of me!—But you never got the card!
SIR GREGORY. What did you do with it?
BENT. I ate it.
OLIVER. Was that the night he left?
BENT. It was like the ringing of the fire engines crowding down the street. There was a sense of something dreadful somewhere.
SIR GREGORY. Did she cry when I was gone?
BENT. She was in a hurricane of temper. Cry she might have done. But I didn't see it.
SIR GREGORY. (*Tenderly.*) Did you cry?
SHE. I wept oceans. But my temper kept me going. Well, let him carve the turkey.

(BENT *pulls himself together and walks with shaky dignity to the console table, examines the turkey, turns to count the number of people.*)

BENT. (*Mutters.*) No need to ease out the legs. . . . There'll be sufficient with the breast alone. (*Picks up carving knife and long steel and sharpens the knife, a little vaguely.*)

OLIVER. (*To* BENT.) Whose name was on the card?

SHE. Get on with that turkey!

BENT. (*Querulously.*) Don't hurry me! I nearly can't do it. . . . (*Drops the carving knife. As he picks it up he makes an extraordinary noise like the bark of a dog beginning with "B."*)

SIR GREGORY. What's that?

SHE. A word one can't say. He says it often.

ALICE. (*To the* BOXER.) Come on, Red Gus—give me a hand.

(*The* BOXER *gets to his feet and lumbers to stand beside* ALICE *near* BENT.)

OLIVER. (*Crossing hurriedly to her bedroom.*) Do you mind if I telephone?

SHE. Yes, I do.

(*But* OLIVER *disappears as though* SHE *hadn't spoken.*)

SIR GREGORY. (*Taking this in—with a half-smile to her.*) Who's *he* in love with?

SHE. His wife.

SIR GREGORY. (*Joining group near* BENT.) That's one mercy!

BENT. (*Who is carving—now pauses. To* SIR GREGORY.) I know who you are now! It's come back to me.

SIR GREGORY. Does it make any difference?

BENT. That's what I've been thinking. It doesn't!

ALICE. Get on, Bent!

BENT. (*Abandoning the carving. Turning to* SIR GREGory.) And if it doesn't—who are we? I mean, I don't know why we have names. (ALICE *gets round him as he talks and gets hold of a filled plate.*) I seem to see more than I used to see! Call it auras. But auras is a lot of nonsense! I get *glimpses!*—I know who you are by your naked soul—hanging where your face should be! (*Brandishes the long knife with the steel almost in* SIR GREGORY'S *face.*)

SIR GREGORY. Pay attention!

BENT. —But I've no name for it.—Perhaps I'm near death.

SIR GREGORY. Cut more slices, Bent. *Keep* cutting. Always employ your hands when you catch yourself thinking about death.

BENT. (*Carving again.*) Oh, I don't look death straight in the face. But sometimes he gets round and looks at me. (*Putting two slices onto a plate.*) Like that, Sir Gregory?

SIR GREGORY. (*Taking the plate to his* WIFE—*the* BOXER *follows, having lifted the mustard pot off the small silver tray it was on.* ALICE *takes the tray and gives it to him, but he holds the tray in one hand and the pot in the other. Taking the* BOXER'S *hands and, as it were, "mating" them so that the pot is on the tray.*) Like that! (*The* BOXER *stoops to offer the mustard.*) What do you do with your money?

BOXER. (*In "stoop-difficulty."*) Buy things.

(SHE *takes an unconscionable time helping herself to mustard.*)

SIR GREGORY. Who advises you?

BOXER. (*Back nearly broken.*) I've got six of 'em. (*At last upright again.*) Very clever tax gentlemen. They work out the dodges.

SIR GREGORY. Put some in my companies.

BOXER. What I like is loose money.

SHE. So does everyone! (*Patting the chair next her.*) Sit down and talk to me!

SIR GREGORY. (*Leaning down to her.*) Are you happy?

SHE. I'm *basking!* (*To* BOXER.) If you've got a girl—buy her diamonds!

BOXER. I haven't got a girl.

SHE. You *haven't!*

BOXER. When I fight I'm not allowed them. (*Mumbling.*) I have to save things.

SHE. (*At a loss.*) *What* things?

BOXER. To keep my mind off them.—A girl would have to be—*extra*—to knock me!

(*Now the hall door opens and* ROXANE *comes in hurriedly. She is breathtaking. Long evening dress; very personal; the effect exquisite. She has dyed her hair since we last saw her—in various shades of bronze, gold and buttercup. It hangs down like a child's. The* BOXER *slowly rises to his feet with tray and pot. He is hit for six. Perhaps forever. He never takes his eyes off her. She half crosses the stage—no doubt a bit guilty about not having been here in the morning, being late now, and perhaps alarmed and dubious about the bottle of gin.*)

ROXANE. (*Not seeing* SIR GREGORY.) Happy Birthday, Mama!

SHE. (*Icy—the battle is joined.*) Why did you send me gin?

ROXANE. (*Halted; reincased in reserve and politeness.*) You spoke about my hair.

SHE. For or against it? (*This is a duel.*)

ROXANE. You don't understand. . . . A girl's hair . . . (*Now she sees* SIR GREGORY. *He is silent. She is silent.*) A girl's hair . . . is like her soul waving! (*Slowly turning her face to her* MOTHER-IN-LAW.) It's something personal and not yet said!—And may *never* be! It's like her handwriting!

SHE. In my day we just had it brushed and arranged. It wasn't this burning, vulnerable, yes-or-no to success.

ROXANE. But in *our* day it's our signature-tune! If it isn't—we're lost!—There are so many of us! All trembling to live!—Most of us trembling. . . . (*To* SIR GREG-ORY.) What are you doing here?

(OLIVER *comes in from bedroom.*)

SIR GREGORY. I'm the husband and the father—"here."

ROXANE. (*To* HER.) I thought he was dead.

SHE. (*Deceptively casual.*) I have revived him.

ROXANE. (*A step further into the room.*) I love a bombshell.—He picked. me up in Bruton Street yesterday near the evening.

TARVER. (*Behind her.*) What do you mean—picked you up?

ROXANE. (*Not turning.*) It's well known—the expression.

OLIVER. (*Hotly.*) Not to *me!*—About *you!*

SHE. This party has exploded in my face! (*To her* HUSBAND.) Did you know who she was?

SIR GREGORY. Of course I didn't! We walked the length of Bruton Street. No more—on my honour! Cairo, Mwelta, Israel—I never saw such a girl! She seemed, even as she walked, to know men wanted her, and be sorry for them.

ROXANE. I don't like things *said!*

ALICE. No, but you do them!

SHE. Roxane—come here to me. (ROXANE *crosses to her. Deliberate.*) Sir Gregory—though my husband—is perfectly free. (*Pause.*) I should have thought you were *not.*

ROXANE. But I want to be.

SHE. Well—I've tried patience and abdication!

ROXANE. (*Slight smile.*) They aren't for you, Mama! I shouldn't try them!

SHE. Do you want to leave us?

ROXANE. Yes.

(*No one had quite expected that flat answer.*)

SHE. And—Oliver?

ROXANE. I'm fond of Oliver but I don't want to be.

OLIVER. Couldn't you have said that first—alone—to me?

SHE. No, because she has brought her life—into my drawing room.

ROXANE. Poor Oliver.

OLIVER. Poor Oliver is *not* what I want to be!

SHE. What do you want, Roxane?

ROXANE. I want to be . . . (*Hunts for a word.*) thought more of!

SHE. So did I! But there's no short cut! It took my life to achieve it.

SIR GREGORY. (*A bit mealy-mouthed.*) And now she deserves respect.

(*His* WIFE *throws a sharp look at him: not pleased.*)

ROXANE. I don't know whether by respect you mean admiration!—Women grow downhill!—I'm at the top! If I can't get it now—when do I get it?

SIR GREGORY. (*Not quite able to resist her.*) What are you at the top of?

ROXANE. My good looks.—It's all I have of my own.

BENT. (*Without emphasis.*) Oh, she's pretty.

(ROXANE *gives a tiny bow.*)

SHE. What can you want—more than that Oliver adores you!

ROXANE. (*Low.*) It's not enough.

OLIVER. (*To his* MOTHER—*with anger.*) Leave that to me! (*To* ROXANE.) *Where* have I failed you!

ROXANE. It's not your fault. But I have to have more . . . (*Stops.*)

OLIVER. More what?

ROXANE. (*Humbly—hanging her head.*) . . . men around me. (*He makes a small exclamation of pain.*) You know those things—stuck to rocks . . . that wait for the sea. . . .

OLIVER. (*Who can never resist her loss of a word.*) Sea anemones.

ROXANE. Yes.—I'm only alive when the tide comes in and men admire me.

SHE. (*Sweeping to sideboard.*) *Uneatable.*

ALICE. Oh, Roxy—how *yourself* you are—absolutely! With your own laws . . . and your own innocence . . .

SHE. . . . But your own manners! (*Putting her untouched plate down.*)

OLIVER. (*Harsh.*) So even an old man . . .

ROXANE. Old men know better what they are admiring. (*Slips her little hand through* SIR GREGORY'S *arm.*)

OLIVER. *Take your hand away!*

ROXANE. (*Obeying.*) It meant nothing!—He's nice to women. Oh—if you hold on to me you'll find—suddenly—nothing, *nothing*, in your hand!

BENT. Oh, she's pretty.

ROXANE. *Can't* you understand me?

OLIVER. Not without pain.

ROXANE. But I don't want to have remorse or sorrow! —I want to go out floating in my best dress in the streets in the early morning—not responsible to anyone—not responsible to you! The happiness I shall get is the looks of the men and the being the fountain for everything! I'm only the breath that—makes the flute play!—And I can only make the flute play—for strangers! (*She moves, hypnotised, towards the* BOXER *as she moves towards him.*)

SIR GREGORY. Have a little decency! Things have to be impalpable!—Not on a Tuesday or a Wednesday—but on some day never named in the week! In my day things had to have mystery! *Unthinkable . . . discussing* it. . . .

ROXANE. (*Low—to* BOXER.) Have you a match?

(*The* BOXER *looks wildly round—no matches.*)

ALICE. In our day . . . (*Mercifully the* BOXER *finds matches and lights* ROXANE'S *cigarette.*) we discuss *everything!*

SIR GREGORY. Do you think a million years have gone by—to arrive at *your* day!

TARVER. That's *just* what she thinks! (*Carries his empty plate, passing* ALICE, *back to the sideboard.*)

ALICE. (*Holding out hers.*) Take mine—

TARVER. Carry your own.

SHE. Oh, Alice! Oh, Tarver! This was meant to be a night with a difference! I had meant to bring the Past into the Present! But back—back—back we go, Gregory, to you and me!

SIR GREGORY. Nonsense!

SHE. The same chemistry! The same sparks and flashes!—And the fire as hard to put out as it used to be!

ALICE. Did you never think that there would be a wife?

SHE. You never crossed my mind when he was young! —But life goes on and I accept you.—I love my sons. And even the girls they married. But I should love them better if their marriages were broken!

ROXANE. (*Softly inserting.*) Alice! Shall we give her back her sons?

ALICE. Give her back!—Leave *Tarver!* . . . —When I hear you talk—as really I never have before—you might be an ant, with an ant's language! Or a silver mackerel! Or a hare from the North Pole! I'm a *woman*. If I leave Tarver it will be with agony! And a need to tear him to pieces—and come back and *look* at the pieces!

SIR GREGORY. (*To* TARVER.) She'll fight you to a stand-still—

ALICE. (*Shouting.*) Yes, I will!

SIR GREGORY. Well, fight her to her knees!

ALICE. (*Rounding on him.*) Tarver and I have each married people with not one thing in common. . . .

TARVER. Nothing, nothing that we agree on! (*To* ALICE.) You are not my type nor my kind of good-looking! You are a badly dressed girl and I hate a badly dressed girl! You argue, you are not accurate and if I ask you the time you tell me the wrong time—

ALICE. (*Furiously.*) And if you marry again you'll

choose the same wife again with the stupidity of a buffalo!

SIR GREGORY. (*Getting up.*) My God, what a house of baboons! (*As he crosses room to the bedroom door. Observing the locked looks of the* BOXER *and* ROXANE.) *Look out, Roxane!—Look out for that man!* He's got to fight in four days! (*Opening the door.*) Shut the current off, girl! It's not fair to him! (*Disappears through door, leaving it open.*)

TARVER. He seems to remember his way about.

ALICE. It must be pleasant to reach that age when one can go to the lavatory without explanation.

SHE. (*Who has been floating, restless and impatient, about the room—now returns to her chair.*) There are many pleasant things aboue age, but listening to the young is not one of them.

(OLIVER *bangs the door shut ferociously.* SHE, *having closed her eyes, gives a start.*)

TARVER. (*Ruefully—to* OLIVER.) I'm thinking of his company—in which I hold a high position!

OLIVER. Well, it wasn't you who banged the door on him!

BOXER. (*In a heaven of his own. Staring into* ROXANE's *eyes.*) A chap has thoughts. . . .

ROXANE. (*Same heaven.*) What are they?

BOXER. That you're as pretty as a little moon on its first night out.

OLIVER. How *dare* you!

BOXER. (*Astonished that there is anyone else in the room.*) What—me?—The very first words I've spoke!

OLIVER. You could keep them to yourself!

BOXER. It seems a pity. I had it in my head and the words flew out.

ROXANE. (*Softly—to* OLIVER.) You have to change men *all* the time.—Don't you *see?*

OLIVER. *No.*

ROXANE. (*Sighing.*) It would be so clear to a woman!

ALICE. No, Roxy. It's not clear to me!—You are very extraordinary—only you don't know it!—It must have cost you the earth to come out into the open! I've hardly ever had a crack out of that lovely secret mouth! (*Suddenly facing* TARVER.) I *talk* when I'm in pain! So that I can *bear* the pain! I *shout!*

SHE. (*Restlessly altering her position.*) Now we have the other one.

ALICE. (*Disregarding—to* TARVER.) I shout! But you don't answer! And when you don't answer I rebel like murder! Oh—that little ounce more of hate that's needed!

BENT. (*Fetching a dirty plate.*) But none of 'em dare.

TARVER. (*Jumping up.*) I've had enough of it!

(SHE *opens her vanity case.*)

ALICE. Back to the flat, then, Tarver! Oh, these flats, oh my God, where there's no room to hate!

SHE. (*Considering her features in the glass of the little case.*) A look of age has appeared in the last five minutes.

ALICE. I ran out into the street yesterday after the row between us—I ran *counting!* Counting the cost of what I'd have to pay in remorse!

SHE. Are there no new lines for two people in anger? I'm appalled at what you *feel!*

ALICE. Well, that's being old.

SHE. It seems to me God knows more reasonable! I should think I was nearer the Almighty and His Everlasting Conundrum than two people wrapped in madness like white silk cocoons!

ALICE. But Tarver and I are not near the Almighty by forty or fifty years! And we have to settle something and with whom to pass the time!

SIR GREGORY. (*Appearing.*) The bathroom has become very feminine! (*Walking over to his* WIFE.) Asleep? (*SHE turns her head and looks up.*) It seems to me that you were asleep.

SHE. (*Bolt upright.*) It seems to me that I am being used up and wasted!—Asleep!—I was *not* asleep! You said it was a house of baboons! But the lions are roaring! I close my eyes—but my ears grow more sensitive! I close my ears but I feel them in my toes!—ASLEEP!— I'm in the Zoo!

ALICE. You don't do much for the animals!

SHE. I can love a human being but I can't love a battle!

ALICE. You can tell us how it can be won!

SIR GREGORY. I can tell you who will be defeated!

ALICE. What *is* this puzzle—that's so well known and never solved! What is this ghastly *difference* between men and women?—What is this closeness that works—and doesn't work! That boils, that burns and blisters, and is so *near* love!

TARVER. (*Sarcastic.*) You call that love?

ALICE. I shan't call it that twice—if you can't see it!— Do you know, Tarver—one word would change our life!

TARVER. What is the word?

ALICE. (*Desolate.*) There are several that might do. It would have to be a light word—like idiot, or . . . It would have to be said with indulgence . . . or . . . humour. It would have to be said without a rifle at my breast. Just saying "idiot" won't do. I don't want it said with pity. . . . (*Suddenly turning to* HER.) You're his mother! Can't *you* tell me what to do!

SHE. You ask advice of my heart—but you know you will throw it back unused!—No, I *can't* tell you!

ALICE. What's the point of being here seventy years— unless age gets you somewhere?

SHE. It doesn't.—*I* made a mess of things.—And now so do you.

TARVER. And what about me! You isolate me! You defend Alice—because it's yourself you're defending!

ALICE. You must come down one side or the other!

SHE. Whatever side I come down—I find I am left alone on it! Roxane is leaving Oliver! I am to see his pain. You and Tarver fight like street dogs. I am torn again! There is *nothing* I can do! Oh—when I had you growing round my skirts it was, as you said, a club! I spun a web—of things we laughed at together! I *knew* your secret wit and chuckles of delight. . . .

OLIVER. And now you know your sons—better than they know their wives.

SHE. (*Stabbed with pain.*) Oliver! (*Hitting back in self-defense.*) I *said* it was wrong—to make friends with the next generation!

TARVER. No, it isn't!—But you use us simply to fill your days!

SHE. I *live* for my children! (*To* ALICE.) Is that wrong?

ALICE. (*Forced to be honest as usual—slowly.*) You can't always be right.

OLIVER. You've woven a habit in us that you can't just break like that!

SIR GREGORY. Take care, my girl! Don't listen to him! Women who outstay their motherhood—become damn boring women! Pale faces looking back into the nursery —like faces in a pond! Leave that to the wives of the Arabs . . . empty as bags! Unfit to be companions! Unfit for anyone!

SHE. (*Her face lighting up.*) Gregory!

SIR GREGORY. (*With energy.*) And what's more—it's a self-indulgence! (*More energy.*) And what's more—it destroys the children!

OLIVER. We can look after ourselves, Sir!

SHE. I'm not sure that you can!

SIR GREGORY. Let them get on with their own lives! I came back to find my wife! Not the mother of my sons!

SHE. It only needed a touchstone to explode! (*To* AL-ICE.) I have been in as many scrapes as you and as many fixes and I have *never* discovered what to do! If I knew, I wouldn't tell you because it may be I don't want to make you happy! Every time I help either of you women to happiness I am helping my sons away from me! It's graceless in you to think I can turn into an advisor be-

cause I am seventy! I wish there was another adventure
for me and, good God, there may be! But not while I
am pulled down by the pressure on me of what you think
I am! In your very manner as you speak to me another
minute is added to my age and taken from my confidence!
I begin to walk slowly because of you. I could skip if I
chose! I could run if I chose! But there is something in
you that dreads that I should seem young, that deplores
it! I don't know what I am doing here at seventy being a
mother!—The *sheep* knows better than that and the *ti-*
gress knows it!

SIR GREGORY. Bravo!

SHE. But is it bravo? Have I been a woman playing
with toys? (*Pause.*) *Should* one live forever for one's
children? (*Pause.*) And their children? For *their* children? Then when does a creature set its *own* house in
order? If not at seventy, when does she do it?

SIR GREGORY. I want you to pack.

SHE. *Tonight!*

SIR GREGORY. Yes. Have you a maid?

SHE. Good heavens, one can't get them!

SIR GREGORY. Then I'll help you. . . .

SHE. Like that! *Now!*

SIR GREGORY. (*Opening bedroom door.*) It's the only
time to do it.

SHE. (*Looking round.*) The house . . . and its lifelong
things . . .

(BENT *seems to try to get up; but can't.*)

SIR GREGORY. . . . will be dust-sheeted. (*Something
about his prompt authority ravishes* HER.) I shall take
you away to Mwelta.

SHE. (*Low—conspiratorially to* OLIVER.) It might be
. . . the Chinese Prime Minister. . . . (*Her hand fingering the birdcage. To* SIR GREGORY.) Do we go up into the
mountains together?

SIR GREGORY. (*Slightly at a loss.*) Well—the hills are
enormous. (*Shrugs.*) But float as though they were light!
—Take one suitcase only.

SHE. Can't I get all I want from the Arabs? (*Going towards door.*) The resolve's very light—so the baggage had better be!—My *make-up* box! (*Goes through door.*)

SIR GREGORY. (*Calling after her.*) And your jewellery!

BENT. (*In his chair. Desperate.*) *I can't sit here and see it happen!* (*Struggles to get up, but can't.*) It'll be the same thing. . . . M'lady . . . m'lady . . . all over again! (*Struggles again to get up. He doesn't see that* SHE *has heard him and is now in the doorway behind him. She wears her sables. Carries long blue gloves, and her make-up box.*) Sir Gregory and Her Ladyship were like two wild animals fighting. The ground was all over blood and hair! The first words came up like lighted matches! The room was on fire before you could turn round! I can't get up. . . .

SIR GREGORY. We won't come back this way—till you have gone. Wiser not to see her again. We must blow out of this house like an explosion—if she's to come! Arrangements and plans and alternative plans. . . . (*To* TARVER.) Send me on bills and I'll settle them. I leave the hard work of the care of the house to you, Tarver. (*Suddenly seeing that his* WIFE *is leaning over* BENT.) You're not packing!

SHE. (*Looking intently down at* BENT, *who is strangely still.*) He's asleep!

SIR GREGORY. (*Looking.*) Are you sure?

SHE. (*Note of panic.*) Tarver! (TARVER *comes up.*) Take his pulse. . . .

(*And it is true that* BENT *is in a very odd position. They are all suddenly still in the presence of death.* TARVER *picks up the old man's cuff and feels his pulse.*)

TARVER. (*As they wait with bated breath.*) None. (*Pause.*) None at all.

SHE. (*Leaning closer.*) So that's death. No sound.—No pain.

ALICE. You are thinking of yourself!

SHE. Everyone's death is a sample of the medicine we'll

soon be taking. (*A note of fear.*) I feel the threshold!
Gregory . . . (*Looking round for his support. As he
comes up to her.*) Oh, what bad timing! (*Leaning over.*)
Bent!—I must *beg* you to live again!

(BENT *stirs.*)

BENT. I've been dreaming.
SHE. We thought you were ill.
BENT. No, you didn't.—And now I know what will
happen. No sooner dead than your minds will be trotting
away from me. And then galloping. But I'm not dead
now!—And to see your faces and your warm living bodies
and the shine on the silver like I never saw before . . .
(*Looks searchingly round.*) and the most beautiful young
thing of all . . . (*Closes his eyes again. In a tired voice.*)
She was pretty.
OLIVER. (*Sharp—strangled.*) *Where's Roxane!*
SIR GREGORY. (*Half aside.*) And where indeed is that
Boxer?
BENT. (*Opening his eyes.*) I frightened her. And it *was*
a near thing! I felt the wonder!—If someone cut my
throat and I died this minute—I'd have *lived*—like a
spark of crystal!
SHE. This decides me. . . . (*Interposed.*)
BENT. (*Gets to his feet. Stumbles towards the hall
door.*) Let me get home—while I feel it!
SHE. (*Anxious.*) Hadn't you a coat?
BENT. (*Walking straight on.*) No.
OLIVER. Shall I call a cab?
BENT. (*Walking on.*) No. (*At the door.*) Good night—
good night. . . . This doesn't come to everyone. (*Goes.*)
SHE. Go after him, Tarver! No coat! And like that!
He might die in the street. . . .

(TARVER *goes towards the door.*)

ALICE. (*Wrought up.*) *Tarver! Wait!* (*He doesn't look*

round.) Tarver! . . . Forgive me!—It was *love! Be* merciful! . . . If you were once merciful . . . If it were once not taken all out of me . . .

TARVER. (*Looking at her.*) Every farthing of your beastliness?

ALICE. . . . so that I lie awake hating myself and hating you for hating myself . . . (*Out he goes. Louder in the hope it may reach him.*) and hating my weakness as I sail to perdition. . . .

SHE. *Alice!*

ALICE. (*Wildly—as she goes.*) I'm for *one* man—even though I hate him. . . . (*Goes.*)

SHE. *Nothing* stops them! They'd quarrel through my funeral. . . .

SIR GREGORY. (*Hard—to* OLIVER.) Where's that chap? (*Pause. Harder.*) Where's your wife?

OLIVER. (*Bitter.*) Away.—Changing men.

SHE. Gregory . . .

SIR GREGORY. (*Peremptory.*) Don't upset your mother!

OLIVER. And lose *both* ways? *Both* women?

SIR GREGORY. You're a mother's son!—Face it. Solve it— You should have solved it sooner!

SHE. (*Expostulatory.*) *Gregory!*

SIR GREGORY. (No.—Let *me* talk to him. (*To* OLIVER.) You've lost your wife. You must decide why.—And whether you want to find her. (*Putting out a hand to stop an impending interruption. To* OLIVER.) It's your affair. Don't talk it over.—*Do* something.

SHE. (*Handing make-up box to her* HUSBAND. *Suddenly frantic. To* OLIVER.) You're not going! (SIR GREGORY *stoops and picks up something.*) You're *not* to go!— Come to the airport!—I can't have this on my mind! I shall be haunted! Oliver!—*Say* something!

OLIVER. Disagreeable as it is—disagreeable as I find him—I shall take his advice, Mother. (*Goes.*)

SHE. (*Instantly flaming.*) You hate him!

SIR GREGORY. I don't hate men. I manage them.

SHE. You're *worse!* You're more tyrannical than ever!

SIR GREGORY. (*Instantly.*) *Then don't come!* (*Looks at her like a man of iron, then, like a small boy, bangs the make-up box violently on the table.*)

SHE. (*A little scream.*) The *bottles!*

SIR GREGORY. (*Opening lid—sheepish.*) Nothing's broken.

SHE. (*Looking inside.*) My *face*—I couldn't go without it! (*Suddenly abandoning this line, looking up at him.*) Are we mad! . . . Is this my second folly? (*He looks down at her.*) Aren't we too old for warfare? (*His face is inscrutable. No doubt he too has a few doubts.*) What shall I *do?*

SIR GREGORY. (*Neutral voice.*) Toss a coin. (*Fishes in a pocket.*)

SHE. (*Watching him, fascinated.*) So . . . clever with your fingers! . . . Naturally . . . (*Her eyes follow coin in air.*) you'll make it come down. . . .

SIR GREGORY. (*As the coin has descended he has put one hand over the other. Removing the hand.*) Heads. (*Looking at her with a faint smile.*) We go.

SHE. (*Uncertain—moving about the room. Pouncing on the birdcage.*) You must take *this!* (*Holds it out to him.*)

SIR GREGORY. (*Aghast.*) Carry *that!*—Take that damn thing!

SHE. Or I don't come!

SIR GREGORY. (*Reaching for it. Under his breath.*) Women . . . (*But he marches to the hall door, birdcage in one hand, make-up box in the other.*)

SHE. (*Hunting about the room—here—there . . .*) I've lost a glove. . . . I've only got one glove! (*He turns, puts birdcage on a small table. Rebell ously.*) I won't go! I *can't* go—without the other one! (*Without a word he draws the second long glove slowly from his pocket and holds it up. She walks across the room and takes it. He picks up the birdcage.*) Are you so certain of me?

SIR GREGORY. No.

SHE. Are you certain of yourself?

SIR GREGORY. No.

SHE. Is it forever?

SIR GREGORY. (*A half smile.*) We'll see. (*Turns and walks out. She follows him.*)

CURTAIN

ACT THREE

Probably late afternoon. The same room, but under white dust-sheets. The strangest disorder. The oddest light-ing. Broken light in shafts crosses the room from a Venetian blind which hangs down in a "fan"—its cord hooked up on one side but free on the other. White linen blinds pulled down. A look of twilight-in-daytime. The chandelier has a linen dust cover. The dust-sheets are scuffled. Have cats or panthers been in here?

The BOXER wanders in in the half darkness. Gazes round. Sees no one.

BOXER. Was it *this* room that night—that had all that light?—It looks like a graveyard. . . .

BENT. (*Removing a bit of dust-sheet from his face. He is lying completely covered by sheets on the sofa.*) Am I dreaming? (*Stares at the ceiling.*)

BOXER. No more'n I am. (BENT *turns his head and sees him.*) Have they quit—the lot of them?

BENT. (*Swinging his legs off the sofa, his knees still covered with the dust-sheet.*) She'll be back! My Lady! With or without her gentleman! Fifty to one. . . . (*Chuckle.*) *Sixty* to one—they'll split.

BOXER. Split?

BENT. What the lightning does to the rock. (*Suddenly alive to situation.*) *Who let you in?*

BOXER. You left the street door open.

BENT. (*Vigorous.*) That's a lie! (*A small doubt.*) The lock's weak. (*Shuffles towards hall door.*)

BOXER. I rang the bell here yesterday.

BENT. (*Complacent—not to say ecstatic.*) I heard it. (*What a pleasure to have chosen not to answer it.*)

BOXER. I saw that girl . . . (*Goes to the window with the plane tree and looks into the leaves, but it is too*

64

dense.) wandering down here back of this house day before yesterday. She went into some gate. That's what I came for! Someone ought to look after her.

BENT. If it's young Mrs. Oliver—it's *your* affair!

BOXER. (*With sudden violence.*) Yes, it is! It's my whole career! I lost that fight because of her! She drove me mad! She's *poison.*—She don't undertake . . .

BENT. (*A tiny thin passion like an insect.*) I'd knock you down if I was young!

BOXER. (*Bitterly.*) Oh, God, that isn't the answer! Knocking people down! It's *me* that's down—down for the count! It's me that's crashed. And all those chaps humming round me wanting me autograph—like smoke they've gone! I'm *out.* D'you know what they said to me? That I'd gone into that fight like a piece of old mutton.

BENT. Pah! *Women!*

BOXER. I hope to God I never see one again. Three days did all that mischief! (*Gloomily.*) I was a virgin.

BENT. (*Deprived of speech for a moment.*) You give me the pip.

BOXER. (*Violently.*) SEX!—They warned me!—A breathless mass of blood and lumps—that's what it's done to me!—*Me!* That's hammered my way through sixty wins in nine years from Liverpool to Utah!—Crazy I was for her! Took her round the town, never went near the gymnasium, slammed down the telephone on the manager!—And then what! *Then* what!—What did that two-fisted bacon-slaughterer do to me!—A demolition-job! *Sex!*—If I'd known what would happen I'd have fled to the Altar!

BENT. (*With deep contempt.*) You chaps that got religion!

BOXER. (*Innocent astonishment.*) Haven't you?

BENT. (*Stooping to attend to his bits of crockery on a tray.*) Me?—I'm *there.* I'm *in* it. Me and the Lord walk up and down this room. (*Suddenly.*) Voices down there! . . . (*Listens.* BOXER *starts to go to hall door.*) Not *that* way! Get out the back. . . . (*Points to pantry door.*)

BOXER. (*Obeying him—muttering as he goes.*) It isn't

that *I* want her . . . (*On exiting.*) But it's my *good deed.* . . . (*He is gone.*)

(BENT *hides under dust-sheets. Enter the* LADY FROM ARABIA *in travelling things.*)

SHE. (*Wandering in.*) The end of Arabia. . . . The end of the flight. . . .

BENT. (*Starting up—indignant.*) You never *said* you were coming!

SHE. (*Unsurprised.*) My old house dog . . . what are you doing here?

BENT. I came to die here.

SHE. (*Indulgent.*) Why in the drawing room? Have you forgotten that you left me?

BENT. I found the key of the back door in my pocket.

SHE. *That* doesn't turn Time back. . . . How long have you been here?

BENT. Five months. (*To her—with strange joy.*) Five months of my own—what I never had before!—The sun and the moon passing over me. . . . And nobody saying to me the dinner's ready—nor the morning's come!—And it isn't being *alone* that makes the difference!—It's being alone—*without Time!* (*Suddenly—taking in that* SHE *seems alone.*) Didn't it do?

SHE. (*Very straight.*) No. It didn't.

BENT. *That* was a mistake—you going! He's mortal meat! (*As* SIR GREGORY *comes in.*) You're *not.*

SIR GREGORY. (*Astonished.*) Why are you here, Bent!

BENT. I'm caravanning.—I mean I'm squatting.

SIR GREGORY. That's what it looks like! Have you fallen out with your wife?

BENT. Fallen foul. You know how it is in marriage, Sir Gregory.

SIR GREGORY. No, I don't.

BENT. (*Sly.*) I've *seen* you knowing!

SIR GREGORY. That's enough! Clear a chair. Bring a chair up. (*Looking round.*) Everything so unready. . . .

We're ahead of the cables, perhaps. We have come back to sell the house, Bent.

BENT. Sell the house . . .

SIR GREGORY. We're going to travel.

BENT. Whatever for?

SHE. The idea is Sir Gregory's.

BENT. (*Suddenly agonised.*) And what about the plane tree? Would they cut it down? There's voices in the plane tree—evenings. I hear things.

SHE. Are you ill, Bent?

BENT. Wearing thin.—And you don't have to be holy to hear them. Any old chap that's wearing thin—if he keeps still enough—can hear a chap speaking.

SIR GREGORY. Is he talking about God?

BENT. No, I'm *not* talking about God.—There's other things in heaven.

SIR GREGORY. That reminds me! I've never checked the luggage! (*Goes out.*)

BENT. (*Muttering.*) Cut the Mother of God out of the branches! It couldn't be done! (*To her—direct.*) You remember that night I went home—carrying my wonder? She dragged me in the dust!

SHE. Why should she?

BENT. Because like an old fool I had a need to tell! And that night I was stuffed with rare stuff—hard to come by! And only having the relationship of bed—she didnt value it!—So—when at the last lip of my time—this *woman*— (*Stops.*)

SHE. (*Startled.*) Bent! What have you *done!*

(SIR GREGORY *returns with the suitcase.* BENT *takes it into the bedroom.*)

ALICE. (*Bursting in.*) *Mama!* (*Instantly turning round and shouting through the door.*) She's here! (*Back to* MOTHER-IN-LAW.) We thought it was *tomorrow!—Nothing's ready!* (*Crossing the room in a rush.*) But I'm *first!* I'm first with the news! (*Pause—triumphant.*) I'm going to have a baby!

SHE. (*Involuntarily.*) Not by Tarver!

TARVER. (*Hard on* ALICE's *heels.*) Why not by me!

SHE. Well, I knew there must have been cooperation.—
I left you hating.

ALICE. Lots of babies are got by hating!

SHE. And what about prison?

TARVER. She got let off.

SHE. So there was pull again!

TARVER. (*Kissing his* MOTHER.) Are you pleased—
about the baby?

SHE. Oh, Tarver—dear Tarver—and dear Alice . . .
(*Taking his hand.*) do you think it's the beginning of the
world?

ALICE. For me it is.

SHE. So it was for me.—And isn't it wonderful how
hope is renewed and one can put up with repetition! . . .
With the autumn and the spring—and the foolishness of
tulips who think they are the first ever seen! (SIR GREG-
ORY *stands looking out at the plane tree. Slyly.*) And to
think—even though I was painted by the best men of my
day—my portrait will end up in the *attic* of that baby!

SIR GREGORY. (*Suddenly pulling up another blind. The
room floods with LIGHT. He turns and looks at the
room.*) How charming the room looks—so nearly empty!
(*Pause.*) I'd forgotten the charm of this room! (*Crossing
to his* WIFE.) I can't think . . . *I can't think why we're
selling it!*

SHE. (*Smiling at her own repetition.*) The idea is your
own! (*She picks up a large conch shell.*)

SIR GREGORY. After all . . . there's no pressing need
to travel. . . .

SHE. (*Putting the shell to her ear.*) And I can hear the
sea just as well from here! (*Toying with the shell.*) I was
told as a child—"Jehovah inhabiteth the shell."

SIR GREGORY. (*Blowing up—for no reason—but there
probably is a reason.*) How I hate whimsey! Women love
it! I hate implication . . . without precision. . . .

SHE. I know!

SIR GREGORY. (*Sticking to his new idea.*) *How about one more London Season?*

SHE. One *more?* We never bothered with one!

SIR GREGORY. We should have done!

SHE. I was too busy! It was a bit of a rush getting famous!

SIR GREGORY. It was a bit of a rush getting rich.

TARVER. Why did you sell your companies, Sir?

SIR GREGORY. (*Turning on him instantly.*) Sell!—Who said *sell?*

TARVER. (*Taken aback.*) I'm . . . in one of them.

SIR GREGORY. (*Angrily.*) My God, how they gossip—the underlings!

SHE. (*Alerted.*) Sell?

SIR GREGORY. (*Overriding.*) One doesn't sell—one refloats and reorganizes. . . .

SHE. Is *that* what happened?

SIR GREGORY. (*But he knows.*) When?

SHE. The night of the Sheik's great party. When you suddenly decided to come home!

SIR GREGORY. (*Defensive.*) Why not? The world's our oyster! (*To* TARVER.) So I feathered the nest—and kept the power, my son! Remember to do that!

TARVER. I'll bear it in mind!

SIR GREGORY. (*Significantly.*) And never *repeat!*—Till you're *sure.*—And not even then.

ALICE. Will they be old or young, Sir Gregory?

SIR GREGORY. Who?

ALICE. The people coming.

SIR GREGORY. It's only the Old who are at the top of things! Would you like to sit next the Prime Minister?

ALICE. (*Shaking her head.*) The gap would be too wide between what I am and what he's done. There's something unfresh about fame!—But Mama knows.

SHE. (*With a start—from abstraction.*) What do I know?

ALICE. You told me once that not much could be done with adulation.

SHE. I told you that when I still had it.

ALICE. Do you still miss it?

SHE. (*Absently.*) As one misses love.—Only at odd moments.

SIR GREGORY. (*To* TARVER.) Are you in touch with architects? . . . (*Looking round.*) We must get decorators . . . *swells!* Always go to the top man! I'd never trust my own taste! . . .

SHE. Not even mine!

SIR GREGORY. (*Going to window.*) A lot has happened to taste since we were young! (*Using his umbrella as a measuring rod to test the height of the window seat.*) Personally I'd have the windows lowered. . . .

OLIVER. (*In doorway.*) And why should *you* be measuring the windows with your umbrella? (*To his* MOTHER.) If you meant to come back and live here *together*—why did you telegraph for *me* to come!

SHE. (*Softly.*) Because there's a crisis. (*Even more softly.*) But it's *my* crisis.

ALICE. Ah.

SHE. Why "ah"?

ALICE. Nothing.

SHE. Do you see Roxane?

OLIVER. No. (*Bitter.*) But sorrow doesn't last!

SHE. Yes, it does—it *does*— Is there somebody else?

OLIVER. (*Bitter.*) Yes. And always will be! (*The truth.*) But never another Roxane . . .

SIR GREGORY. There's a young fool—if ever there was one. (*To* TARVER—*tapping on a wall.*) There's a room through this wall we could throw in.

OLIVER. What for!

SIR GREGORY. For large scale entertaining.

TARVER. (*Pointing to the window with the plane tree.*) And the little garden? And the mews cottage—that was the stables?

OLIVER. *I* want it.

SIR GREGORY. What for?

OLIVER. To write in.

SIR GREGORY. (*Offhand.*) Is that what you are—a writer?

OLIVER. Have you something against it?

SIR GREGORY. No. I read books. Though you mightn't think it. But you have to know where you are with a man. I never trust writers, poor devils. It's like sinking a shaft in quicksand.—But on with our plans. (*To* ALICE.) How about a swimming pool—and the mews as a dressing room?

ALICE. If you're altering the house—how about the top floor that's shut?

OLIVER. I suppose it's not struck anybody . . . (*They look at him.*) that my mother plans nothing?

SHE. (*On the periphery, yet lying in wait.*) It seems not to have.

SIR GREGORY. Your mother needs putting back into life!

SHE. (*Softly.*) Whose life?

SIR GREGORY. Mine. (*Searching in a pocket.*) Where's my little book? (*Pulls out his engagement book. Flicking over pages.*) When's the season? . . . May? (*More pages.*) What are we now?

SHE. You're seventy!—And so am I—

SIR GREGORY. (*Startled.*) Why should that make one behave differently!

BENT. (*Returning from bedroom.*) What silly ass wants to do the same things over again!

SHE. (*Suddenly—to* BENT.) Bent,—would you like to see the house alive again?

BENT. It's been so beautiful—dead. Excuse me, M'lady. May I have a moment of your time? (*She looks up in surprise. Is he going to give notice? Yes, he is.*) Might I ask permission to sit down? (*She assents.*) I am afraid I must give my notice.—You remember that night—sitting here—that I nearly died? I have the same feeling on me now. This time I think I shall make it.

SHE. (*Intensely interested.*) *Bent*—are you going to *die?*

BENT. I think I am. (*Pause.*) You'll find it's nothing. (*Pause.*) Most people die murdered.

SIR GREGORY. Good God, what's he mean!

BENT. I mean by disease or some accident. I'm at the age when I'm merely withdrawing. If everybody arrived —where I've arrived—there'd be no fear of death. The legend would be finished. It's like taking trouble . . . over a bubble. . . . (*Pause.*) So few people achieve the final end. *Most* are caught napping. (*Silence. Then shockingly clear.*) *My last advice—M'lady—Don't do things twice!* (*Dies. But adds.*) Put a screen round me. So you can go on talking. (*Dies.*)

SHE. Dear me.

TARVER. Good God.

SIR GREGORY. Is the chap dead?

OLIVER. (*Who has taken his pulse.*) They've snuffed him out like a candle.

SHE. And much left unsaid.

TARVER. We must ring someone!

SHE. Who is there to ring?

SIR GREGORY. We must ring the police!

SHE. And if we don't ring the police for ten minutes, Bent won't tell them. He has told you what to do. Put the screen round him.

SIR GREGORY. You can't *do* such a thing!

SHE. Yes, you can. He'll be dead for so long.—He said the only way to—*enjoy death*—was to— (*Pausing to give emphasis as she slowly chooses her words.*) *exhaust* life! —And not be caught napping!

SIR GREGORY. Have you gone off your rocker?

SHE. (*Nodding at the screen.*) No, but my warning's come! There are things to be seen—that are the things we have always seen—but different! There must be more in the moment itself! And less in the programme. . . . Now that I am without Bent . . . (*They all look apprehensively at the screen.*) He may be playing some trick on me. Go and look.

OLIVER. (*Looking.*) No. Still dead.

SHE. As I was saying—now I am without Bent—there may be *another* way to live. . . .

OLIVER. Then what's all this talk of entertaining?

SHE. He made plans. And I listened.

TARVER. But you let him run on!

SHE. That was my irresolution.

SIR GREGORY. All I ask is to live as I've always done! I'd like every bloody minute of the same thing over again!

SHE. (*Pause.*) Then will you go back to Arabia?—And leave me to try living alone?

OLIVER. You haven't quarrelled again!

SHE. Yes, we have. In the back of the taxi that took us that night—in the plane . . . and—— (*With a sweeping gesture.*) all over the mountains of Arabia!

TARVER. What on earth d'you want to live alone for?

SHE. I want to be attentive to . . . (*Slight smile.*) trivial things.

SIR GREGORY. And weren't you before!

SHE. Never without that guilt—peculiar to women!

SIR GREGORY. How do *I* produce it!

SHE. By being you, Gregory! Women are so dutiful!—And the best men make them work so hard for them!—By the time-table married life imposes . . . by this little book we carry! (*Waving the little scarlet book at him, that she has kept in her hand.*) I have yet to find out what a day is like when I am not planning the next one!

ALICE. I can't imagine not looking ahead!

SHE. That's how I've turned Saturday into Monday and Monday into Saturday—and become seventy!

SIR GREGORY. (*Suddenly intensely irritated.*) They hit you where you can't get 'em—those nebulous answers of women!

ALICE. Mama wants to get free from every responsibility!

SHE. (*Murmuring.*) Except one.

ALICE. Who is on your conscience?

SHE. There is always someone.

ALICE. (*Fiercely.*) I should like to think that it's my unborn son!

SHE. Well, it isn't.

SIR GREGORY. (*Boiling over.*) Get out—the lot of you! Get out—the next generation!

ALICE. What—*me?*

SIR GREGORY. Yes—*you!*—I want to talk to my wife!
(*Waits, glaring as they go out. When the door is shut he
helps himself to a cigarette which he does not light.* SHE
*goes over and looks out of the window. After a pause—a
change in tone.*) So—you don't want to sell the house.
And you don't want to travel. (*Slight smile.*) And you
don't want me here? Is that it? (SHE *turns, saying noth-*
ing.) See if I can understand you! (*Slight laugh.*) I can
understand men!

SHE. Men wouldn't say what I'm saying!—That I
want the whole of myself—and not half again! "I am as
I am!" you used to say. We were so different that when
two rooms separated us for half an hour—we met again
as strangers. It was I who was told to change!

SIR GREGORY. That's a tussle that nobody sees plainly
till they get into the deeps of marriage! Hasn't it worked
—these five months?

SHE. (*Coming near him.*) Has it?

SIR GREGORY. Of course it has! I want a woman with
the faults I know!— (*Coming up to her.*) where I'm either enchanted—or bark my shins on the furniture! . . .
The battle of two people who won't leave each other—

SHE. But you did!

SIR GREGORY. I was wrong.

SHE. You're stout as an old stick one leans on!—You
know we waste each other! But you won't be the first to
say it! We're two old lions when we're together!—The
old answers—to the old vexations! The battle to be
right . . .

SIR GREGORY. And some sort of rule about forgiving?

SHE. Yes. The sun going down. Gregory, it's here we
speak the truth! (*Pause.*) And the heart has no part in it!
—I'm going to be cascaded into eternity! (*Ruefully.*) I'm
more interested in the full moon!

SIR GREGORY. Don't be arrogant, my old girl! You were
always arrogant! There's a ceiling *there* (*Points up.*) and
a floor *there*— (*Points down.*) and no one gets beyond it!
—Not the clever chaps more than the stupid chaps—but
the clever chaps grow paler! (*He walks away a little*—

something on his mind.) That night I came to dinner—
what made you suddenly give in?

SHE. My . . . (*Hesitating.*) my femininity!—I wanted
it confirmed!

SIR GREGORY. Before I came . . . (*Now he pauses to
light his cigarette.*) those tales . . . (*Slight effort.*) that
stuff about a lover! What made you spill the beans?

SHE. They thought I was boasting.

SIR GREGORY. (*Casual.*) And were you?

SHE. Does it matter?

SIR GREGORY. (*Less casual.*) *Were* you?

SHE. (*Mocking.*) Not—on a Tuesday or a Wednesday . . .

SIR GREGORY. (*An old rage.*) You damn maddening
woman! What was that fellow's *name?*

SHE. The singer?

SIR GREGORY. Of *course* the singer.

SHE. Can't you remember?

SIR GREGORY. *No!*

SHE. (*Pause. The incredible truth.*) Well, I can't,
either.

SIR GREGORY. (*Winded.*) It was in *that chair* you told
me!

SHE. (*Fingering the arm of the chair.*) In the momen-
tary hate of love I might have said anything!

SIR GREGORY. (*Menacing.*) Was he your lover?

SHE. (*Simply.*) I had the wish. (*Musing.*) But did it
happen?

(*A pause.*)

SIR GREGORY. (*A sudden roar of laughter.*) So what the
hell do you tell Oliver!

SHE. (*Instantly alarmed.*) Gregory—you'll never—no
matter what happens—or under what circumstances . . .

SIR GREGORY. Throw a doubt?—No, never! God, I'm
glad I've seen 'em!

SHE. (*Can she have heard the plural.*) *Them!*

SIR GREGORY. *Both* of them. Now it's the *plant* that

matters! What a fuss about a seed!—The desire for a
son was only present after seventy. I'm an old egotist.
. . . (*He finds himself in front of the mirror. Pause.*)
What a *monstrous* thing. . . .

SHE. (*Startled.*) What?

SIR GREGORY. *Age* is a monstrous thing! Just when a
man's at the top of life—off they want to tip him!
(*Shakes his fist at the face in the mirror.*) I've learnt the
whole bag of tricks! I know the weakness of a man as
quick as you can feel a drop of rain! I can see in an
Arab's eye which way he's heading! I can feel the flow of
money like a fish in the river! (*Turning round on her.*)
To be old is *magnificent!* But damned if they'll admit it!

SHE. What do you want *most*, Gregory?

SIR GREGORY. You.

SHE. It's too late for gallantry. (*Softly.*) Think again.

SIR GREGORY. (*With sudden violence.*) *I want my own
way!* (*Not looking at her.*) I want what I've always had!

SHE. (*Insisting.*) But . . . most? (*There is no answer.
Then.*)

SIR GREGORY. *Power!—Respect!* (*Bitterly.*) Or *fear*
will do!

SHE. (*Shaking her head.*) Still not the truth. . . .

SIR GREGORY. (*Walks away from her. Turning, violently.*) *Blast* the end of life!—And the way men take it!
(*Halts. Through clenched teeth.*) And *blast* the Sheik!

SHE. (*Low—but he hears.*) I knew it.

SIR GREGORY. (*More quietly.*) He's making ready to
die and he's gone out of my range.—He wants Arabs
about him.

SHE. At the party? Was it *that* night he told you?

SIR GREGORY. Huh! Arabs never tell you things! But
suddenly—there's more dignity and less intimacy—and
your hold's gone! I was to sell my companies. *He* wanted
them. Thirty years we'd been together. Same age as I
am. (*Pause.*) I said I wouldn't. Then he turned his eyes
on me. And his eyes upset me. I flung out of the doors.—I
thought he'd send for me.

SHE. And he didn't.

SIR GREGORY. He sent his emissary. It was that night, yes, I knew what it meant.—It was done in the form of a present. A jackal . . . (*Holding up thumb and finger to show the size.*) in gold and jade. (*Pause.*) I threw it in the sea at Gibraltar when we changed planes. (*Pause.*) Once more the Arabs have disgorged the English! (*Sits down as though his legs have given way.*) I can govern men, my girl!—But I don't know *what* life is about! (*Knowing there are tears in her eyes.*) Take my handkerchief—the top pocket one!—It always ended like this—didn't it?

OLIVER. (*In the doorway. He sees it is a farewell.*) Are you going out of our lives again?

SIR GREGORY. Yes. Are you glad of it?

OLIVER. Oddly enough—no.

SIR GREGORY. I remember you in your cradle—with your writer's eyes screwed up against me!—A mother's son from the start.

OLIVER. *I* had no hand in it. (*Pause.*) Whether you are my father—or not . . .

SIR GREGORY. (*Instantly—a blaze.*) *I am!*

OLIVER. If I may be allowed to say so . . . *Nonsense, Sir!*

SIR GREGORY. You are *not* allowed! You think you know, puppy, why I parted from her!—You think some chap fathered you?—Well, he didn't! When your mother fell in love I knew how to forgive her! It isn't the faults on the grand scale that matter. It's the little fault, the rubbish of life, the damn thing that crops up too often! (*Glares for a moment. Then.*) A million to one you don't know why I left her! I wore *boots. Patent leather.* She swore she had put the laces in and she damn-well knew she hadn't!—The room blew up. I threw my glasses—they broke. She threw her slipper. I shook her chair as she sat and it went over. . . .

SHE. (*Again touching the arm of the chair with her fingertips.*) You *tipped* me over.

SIR GREGORY. Well, whether I did or not I went blazing across the sky to Arabia! (*A sudden impulse. To* OLIVER.) If I go back . . . Come with me!

OLIVER. You have Tarver.

SIR GREGORY. He's too like me! What a man wants is a surprise-packet! (*Chuckling.*) What Joseph must have felt—in Jerusalem! (*Looking and nodding at* OLIVER.) I could do something with you! (*Pause.*) Put that girl out of your mind! (*Pause.*) Do you know where she is?

OLIVER. I have her followed.

SIR GREGORY. What do you hope to gain by that!

OLIVER. Only the sad knowledge that she wants for nothing.

ROXANE. (*Standing in the doorway to the kitchen. In an exhausted voice.*) Or that what she wants—she *has!*

OLIVER. (*Unsurprised.*) Roxane . . .

ROXANE. I came through from the mews cottage. . . . (*Struck by his attitude.*) You didn't *know* I was there!

OLIVER. I knew it.

SHE. (*Low—she understands what Bent heard.*) The voices in the plane tree . . .

ROXANE. (*Using the curious, unaccustomed word.*) Mother . . . in . . . law. . . .

SHE. (*Startled*) You *never* called me that!

ROXANE. It holds me to life a little.

SIR GREGORY. What were you doing there?

ROXANE. I sleep where I can.

SIR GREGORY. Alone?

ROXANE. With a stranger.

SIR GREGORY. (*Indignant.*) Couldn't the chap afford—?

SHE. (*Interrupting—tilting up* ROXANE's *face—tenderly.*) How tired you look. . . .

OLIVER. But pretty!

ROXANE. (*Looking at him a moment.*) Isn't it sad that I should be so pretty . . . (*Low.*) and any man can have me.

SIR GREGORY. Good God, what a thing! What do you get out of it that *one* man can't give you?

ROXANE. Only—saying—"yes."

SIR GREGORY. It seems damn little!

SHE. Roxane . . . Roxane. Who's to look after you!

ROXANE. Nobody. I'm like one of those . . . (*Looks helplessly at* OLIVER, *who has always found her words when they failed her.*) *you* know . . . that die at dusk.

OLIVER. (*Gay—as though it was a game they were playing together.*) *Dragonflies!* (*Moves a small step towards her. She starts back, alarmed.*) Keep still, my love! (*Another step.*) How sweet you look. . . . (*Imperceptibly moving—as though she were a small wild animal.*) don't move . . . keep still . . . how pale. . . . (*Nearer. Close—but not touching her.*) I love your hair like that! —Sweet and untidy!

ROXANE (*A whisper.*) I can't come back.

OLIVER. (*Tenderly, soothing—matching her tone.*) You shan't come back. . . . (*Slips an arm round her gently.*) Is that your waist?—Slender?

ROXANE. (*Lifting her face—murmuring her new truth.*) I have no sex, Oliver.

OLIVER. Nor has a child, my lovely! (*Over her shoulder he puts a finger to his lips—for silence. Moving her gently.*) Where shall we dine? (*Persuading. Stooping to her ear.*) I'm hungry. (*Step by delicate step they go towards the door.*)

ROXANE. (*Stopping a moment.*) How can you be like this?

OLIVER. It's what I was born for.

(*They move on again—and disappear. There is a moment's silence.* SIR GREGORY *crosses the room and shuts the door carefully.*)

SHE. I have escaped by a miracle! *She* is the one! He will forgive me.

SIR GREGORY. To be plain about it—the girl's on the streets. (*Going back to her.*) How can he live with her?

SHE. You can live with anything human.

SIR GREGORY. Then why can't you put up with me?

(*The door bursts open and* ALICE *comes in, holding a yellow envelope in either hand.*)

ALICE. A cable, Sir Gregory!

SIR GREGORY. (*Taking it. Dully.*) Goddamn 'em.

ALICE. And another!

SIR GREGORY. (*Taking the second cable.*) Goddamn 'em twice over. (*Cables in hand, he gets up, slams them down on a table, leans over, glaring at* ALICE.) And who's to see *me* off—as an old man! (*Grim.*) *Has she thought of that?*

(*Pause.*)

SHE. Yes . . . I think of it. . . .

SIR GREGORY. I shall die sooner than you will. (*As he speaks he picks up one of the envelopes.*)

ALICE. (*Cheekily.*) But supposing you don't?

SIR GREGORY. (*Sharp.*) You keep out of it! (*Slitting envelope open. More mildly.*) Threescore years and ten is all they give us! (*Pulls out a three-page cable: one page flutters to the floor.*)

ALICE. But if there's a bit over . . . (*Stoops to pick up the page. Intuitively.*) it's her own.

SIR GREGORY. (*Taking the page from her.*) What should she want to do with it. . . . (*His eye catches something: his voice trails to inattention.*)

SHE. (*Low.*) What should I want to do with it . . . ? (*Moves away. He takes no notice. His hand goes to his coat pocket for his reading glasses, changes glasses, spreads the three pages flat on the table, leans over them, reads. To herself—as he reads.*) I want to find out who I am. I can wear the personality of anyone—why else have I been an actress? Thirty authors—or thirty lovers—have made thirty women of me . . . (*Suddenly—to* ALICE.) How *much* does he need me?

ALICE. He isn't listening.

SHE. (*Watching him—as* ALICE *also watches. Pause.*) What is it, Gregory?

SIR GREGORY. (*Upright. His old eyes blazing.*) *Oil again!* (*Smashing his hands down on the cables.*) Oh, my God—oil again! Where they've never found oil before! And that damned old Moslem kneels and prays to Allah!—

SHE. (*Breathless.*) They want you again. . . .

SIR GREGORY. No pipelines—no anything! My desert bursting—on the far side of the mountains!—"*Want me again*"? They can't do without me! They want a new Concession!

ALICE. Does that mean money?

SIR GREGORY. It *does* mean money! (*Gay, whirling. Opening dispatch case to make sure of wallet, passport, etc.*) They're squealing for money! (*Zips it up again.*) And they know I can whistle up money—with a fortune behind me like mine! (*To* TARVER.) Remember that when you're rich—that money finds money!—And get me a taxi—*quick*. We'll go down to the City. . . .

(TARVER *rushes off.*)

SHE. His coat—Alice! (*She herself picks up hat, scarf, gloves.* ALICE *holds the coat ready.*)

SIR GREGORY. (*Getting into his coat. Struck by a thought.*) And what about you? (*Suddenly turning his head and looking at* HER.) Why don't you travel? Take Bent!— (*Suddenly turning his head and looking at the screen.*) My God . . . I'd forgotten him! (*Exasperated. As* SHE *hands him gloves.*) *Now*—who's to look after you! . . .

SHE. (*Wildly hunting for his umbrella.*) Like the poets and the drunks . . . (*Looks in another corner.*) I shall end the appointment with food— (*Pounces on it.*) and the appointment with dressing. . . . (*Dusts the umbrella with her hand.*)

SIR GREGORY. Very uncomfortable!

SHE. It wouldn't suit a man!

SIR GREGORY. (*Another thought.*) And—come to that . . . you may die yourself!

SHE. I don't think I shall. I can't be bothered with it!

SIR GREGORY. (*At the door—going.*) I shall come back. (*Suddenly opens his arms wide to* HER.)

SHE. (*Smiling.*) Your umbrella, Gregory.

(SHE *pops it into his opened arms. So he kisses, instead of her, the hand that holds it.*)

SIR GREGORY. (*Going through door.*) I'll look in on my way to the plane. (*Disappears.*)

SHE. (*Calling through the open door after him.*) If you have time. . . . (*Waits. Gently closing the door with finality. With a curious triumph.*) He *won't* have time! (*Crosses to window. Now a complete change of manner.*) He is looking forward again! (*Throws up window and waves down.*) But I am going to make Time stand still! (*Turning back into the room.*) It is *I* who am the Chinese Prime Minister!

ALICE. What do you want, Mama?

SHE. To be alone. (*Moving majestically towards the central armchair.*) For after death I shall never know him again. (*Sits down.*) And I may have to know myself. (*Silence. Then:*) You think, Alice, that I have duties. (*Musing.*) And in my way I have done them. But I inherit the dual sex that the centuries have slowly brought me. I am a modern, not an antique woman. And there is a Me in me that I have never conquered.—And don't intend to.—Without it nothing has importance.

ALICE. We are so close, Mama!

MRS. FOREST. Not yet! You are still a woman!—But I am a rock three parts submerged. I shine on the skin of the sea—waving my seaweed. The rock below is common ground. (*Pause.*) Had you thought of living in the top floor yourself?

ALICE. It did occur to me.

SHE. With Tarver—and the baby?—And other babies?

ALICE. Would you like that?

SHE. Would you think it unsuitable if I said no?

ALICE. (*Stung.*) I thought women liked being grandmothers!

SHE. It isn't the grandmothers who say so! The using-up of grandmothers is not for me. It was pre-Christian! Now only the Latins and the natives do it! I admire you, Alice, and I know what's in your mind!—But I won't help you with the nursery, my dearest! I won't fill-in for you with the harness of the kisses at six. I *had* my babies—it was like love! But I won't do things twice! (*Suddenly throwing out both arms to their length—stretching, as though waking.*) Alice!—Above all things . . . I want a cup of tea! (ALICE *slips away at once to the kitchen door. Calling after her.*) Everything must be there—in the kitchen. . . . (ALICE *is now gone. Now* SHE *gets up.*) Free me. . . . (*Pause. Walks up and down.*) From the expectation of tomorrow—free me! From the eye of the clock—free me! From the habits of a lifetime . . . but they are as strong as *harness!*—I shall have to *exaggerate* . . . to get them off in time! (*Looks around the room.*) Let the house burn! Let me not . . . (*Speaking rapidly—counting her fingers.*) Have to remember to turn the gas off, make sure of the insurance, ring for the fire engines, save my jewels!—I will go out into the garden and think how beautiful—are the flames! (*Pause. Seeming to wake up.*) But I can't talk to *nothing!* Even on the stage—one can't do that! Or not in the plays. . . . *I* was brought up to play in!—A second actor makes a dialogue!—Even a dead one! (*She sweeps the light screen to one side. There is time to see that though* BENT *died with his arms hanging at his sides—his hands are now folded in his lap.*) Bent!—are you alive?

BENT. (*Eyes shut.*) Just about.—Hardly.

SHE. (*Murmuring.*) like a watch that one shakes—you've gone on again.

BENT. (*His head tilts forwards; his fingers seem to count his waistcoat buttons.*) Back in the old carcass.—It don't seem to fit. (*Looking up—his eyes now open.*) There's things going on you wouldn't believe!—Like Easter on a farm with the cocks crowing! A whistling—

very old—that I should have heard before.—And cries—
and catcalls—of the gods.

SHE. Where?

BENT. Threading through the traffic. And in the yard.
It's thick as Derby Day. Everything is everywhere. . . .
Even a spoon I'd lost—let alone the people.

SHE. Would you rather have died?

BENT. No, I wouldn't. (*Pause.*) And *I'd* like a cup of
tea.

(SHE *starts, looks at him with suspicion. Crosses to
kitchen door and calls down.*)

SHE. *Alice!* (*Waits.*) Bring two cups. (*Pause.*) Or if
you want one—*three.* (*Walks slowly back, her eyes on*
BENT.) Bent—we are alone.

BENT. (*Shutting his eyes again. Cautious.*) But how
are we sure of anything?

SHE. That night she threw you out—*did something
happen?*

BENT. (*Pause.*) How are we sure? (*Thinks.*) I had the
wish. (*Thinks harder.*) But did I put it into action?

SHE. (*Deep suspicion again.*) My very words!—So one
can eavesdrop from heaven?

BENT. (*Anxious.*) What'll you do?

SHE. (*Moving away—forgetting him.*) Reverse the
habits of a lifetime.

BENT. I mean—about *me?*

SHE. About you?—Nothing. When the unplanned day
is before me . . . (*Stops.*)

BENT. (*In his cunning manner.*) How'll you fill it?

SHE. I shall indulge the pleasures of the senses. (BENT
cups an ear. Can he have heard aright?) Heat and cold—
for instance! And make *sure* I feel them!—Like Alex-
ander—who changed a cold stone from his left to his right
hand, that each hand in turn knew it was living.—I shall
cut down sleep. . . . There are pills to keep you awake,
and I shall take them. . . .

BENT. (*Mutter.*) You may pop off doing that.

SHE. (*Replying automatically—but not to him.*) And
if I die in ten years—or ten minutes—you can't measure
Time.—In ten minutes everything can be felt!—In four
minutes you can be born! Or live.—In two minutes God
may be understood! And what one woman grasps—all
men may get nearer to. . . . (*Pause.*) When I stir my
coffee at dawn . . .

BENT. Who's going to give it to you?

SHE. (*Tart.*) You.—A man who can die twice can do
anything! I shall get up in an ecstasy of no-responsibility
—as though it was the beginning of the world—and toss
the grass with my rhinoceros horn—and be barbed with
words like Saint Sebastian!

(*The door opens.* ALICE, *her eyes glued on the tray she
is carrying, walks in.*)

ALICE. Why the third cup?

SHE. (*Gay.*) Show no astonishment. Take it as a miracle!—There are lots of them! Pour it out. For me—no
sugar. (ALICE *pours, filling two cups.*) I have always been
a punctual woman. I have never glanced at the sea as I
drove to the station. If God had been stoking the engine
I wouldn't have seen Him! There are continents around
and about us . . . (ALICE *takes her own cup and walks
two steps into another life.*) and wild, unharvested
things. . . . (*Fills the third cup.*)

ALICE. (*Hypnotized by her own dreams.*) What . . .
things?

SHE. (*Adding sugar. Gay.*) Why the grey parrot talks
—and not the green! (*Crossing the Stage with the cup,
flinging each line back as she crosses.*) Why a sea lion—
out of the cold sea—can come into a circus and understand fame! How a dog can establish with me the mystery
of humour!—I want to think of these things and find the
springs in common there may be. (*Puts the cup down by*
BENT.)

BENT. I should like to know what happened between
you and Sir Gregory?

SHE. We parted again.

BENT. (*Fishing up a light thought from his crumbled surface.*) I am glad you are back.—You were meant to be a single woman.—For that is how you were born. (*Second light thought.*) And I'm glad for Sir Gregory. Women of individuality—are damned uncomfortable for men.

SHE. And I'm glad you are alive.

BENT. Hardly worth mentioning. I'm an old leaf—from an old tree. And even the tree cut down.

SHE. Oh, Bent—ah, Bent! What did I always tell you! If you hadn't drunk and you hadn't fornicated—what a poet you'd have been!

CURTAIN

PROPERTY PLOT

ACT ONE

PRESET
Furniture:
Large secretary D.L. half off in wings.
Secretary chair R. of secretary.
Oval table in corner above kitchen door L
Sideboard centered against U.L. windows.
Large blue sofa running from C. to D.L. in line with U.L.
   windows.
Coffee table in front of sofa.
Small blue armchair R. of sofa.
Serving table upstage and R. of bedroom door.
Chinese screen masking front door entrance (dull side out).
Small blue chair hidden behind screen.
Small round table with lamp in corner below L. of bookcase.
Small round table with lamp above stage R. window.
Small phone table R. of chaise.
Chaise two feet stage L. of upstage corner of R. window.
Pouf (matching chaise) below chaise.
Grey footstool right of chaise—below stage R. window.
Small table in hall up against stairwell.
Chair just R. of hall table.

PRE-SET ONSTAGE
Yellow curtains—Windowshades all the way up on stage L.
   windows.
Yellow curtains—Downstage R. window.
Yellow curtains—Upstage R.
On phone table:
   Cigarette dish with cigarettes.
   Match holder/ashtray with matches.
   Brass flower pot with small bouquet and card saying, "With
      Love."
   White telephone.
On small table stage R. above window:
   Lamp.
   3 small framed pictures.
   1 small ceramic bird.

Pillows:
   On sofa—three blue matching pillows—one sampler pillow.
   On chaise—one matching brown cushion—lace side out.
On serving table:
   Large vase flowers surrounded on four sides by small pictures.
2 candles in U. R. wall chandelier.
On sideboard:
   Decanter.
   Three drinking glasses.
   Water pitcher.
   2 champagne glasses.
   Clock (in center).
   Champagne bucket with towel inside.
   Gin (almost gone), scotch, whiskey.
On coffee table:
   Ashtray.
   SHE'S purse.
   SHE'S glasses.
   Cigarette box.
On secretary:
   Paperweight.
   Ashtray.
   Small single yellow rose in vase.
   5 playscripts in stamped mailing envelopes.
   Red engagement book.
   Lamp (Upstage end).
On oval table stage L.:
   Lamp.
   Three pictures in frames.
   Small heart-shaped ashtray.
   Small vase of flowers.
   Bird cage (mechanical bird).
   Small decorative paperweight.
In dressing room inside bedroom:
   Small leather makeup case.
   4 stamped (not posted) envelopes.
   TARVER'S note.
In bookcase:
   All books.
   Two small pictures.
Small table beneath bookcase:
   Lamp.
   Three pictures in frames.

Offstage L.:

In Kitchen:

Green tray with sugar, creamer, tea pot with tea, 3 cups, saucers and spoons.

Turkey tray with 10 slices pre-cut, carving knife and fork.

Silver tray with plate, serving sliver dish, spoon, knife, fork, cup and saucer (For I-2).

Small silver tray (I-1 egg tray) with dish with toast and pat of butter, salt and pepper tray, dish with egg in egg cup, glass ¾ full of water, napkin, butter knife and spoon. *Note:* Egg should be 3 minute egg.

3 bottles of champagne (2 real—one mixed ginger ale and water).

Prop Table Stage L.:

Silver tray (round) with four champagne glasses.

Birthday cake with 2 candles.

1 brown paper bag with loose candles and 2 tied up bunches of candles inside.

BENT's watch.

Dust cloth.

Large oval tray with 6 dinner plates, 6 forks, silver polishing cloth, large serving spoon, small silver tray with small mustard pot and spreader, large glass dish fruit salad.

1 English "Mid-day" newspaper.

Stage R. *Prop Table:*

6 cake plates, cake knife, 6 forks.

Wrapped gin bottle (in box) with note stuck to bottle and note on outside box.

Wrapped grocer's package of pâté de foie gras.

2 telegrams (International Cables).

TARVER's umbrella and derby.

Suitcase.

Basket of wilted flowers.

Basket of fresh flowers.

Single yellow rose in silver vase.

PROP CHANGES

STRIKE:

Torn card from ashtray.

Scripts from secretary.

All flowers from set.

RE-SET:
Secretary's chair to face in to secretary.
Gin bottle from I-1 to behind other bottles on sideboard.
Blue armchair to stage L. of chaise—facing pouf.
Heavy drapes on D.R. window.
Telephone—turns to face upstage.
Red engagement book onto phone table.

BRING ON:
Cake to coffee table.
Bag of candles to coffee table.
Wrapped birthday gifts to secretary.
3 champagne bottles to sideboard.
Small single rose in vase to phone table.
6 cake plates, forks and cake knife to serving table.

PROP CHANGES

ACT TWO

STRIKE:
Packages from secretary.
Oval food tray.
Newspaper.
Address/Engagement book.
Dishes, forks, knife.
Umbrella and derby (*Note:* Umbrella strikes Stage R. for SIR
  G).
Champagne glasses and used bottle.
4 stamped envelopes.
All drinking glasses (used).
Champagne bucket.
Gin bottle (gift).
Yellow curtains.

RE-SET:
Phone to I-1 position.
Small chair behind screen to just R. of bedroom doorframe.
Blue armchair to just left of sofa, facing D.L.
Pouf to R. of chaise facing up and downstage.
Serving table downstage to Act II marks.
2 glasses on serving tray on sideboard.
Birdcage to phone table.

BRING ON:

Tablecloth (lace).

Heavy drapes and hang windows L. and R.

Set on serving table: (After setting lace tablecloth).
  Mustard pot on tray (D.L. end table).
  Forks and polishing cloth (L. end table).
  Fruit cocktail in bowl L. end table.
  Turkey on tray (slices on upstage side)—on U.R. end table.
  Carving tools on U.C. end table.
  6 folded napkins (D.R. end table).
  6 dinner plates (D.C. end table).

Candelabra on sideboard.

Clock on sideboard onto windowsill.

3 brandy snifters on sideboard.

Bottle of Hennesy Cognac on sideboard.

ACT III

STRIKE:

Birdcage.

Serving table with food and plates etc.

Silver polishing cloth.

All silverware, dishes, napkins, glasses, plates left on set.

All pictures on tables.

All flowers.

All books from bookcase.

Candelabra.

All candles.

All lamps from tables.

Small lamp table stage R.

Heavy drapes.

All bottles.

Pillow from chaise and lace pillow from sofa.

RE-SET:

Telephone to under telephone table.

Fold screen and place against arch post R. of bedroom door.

Secretary's chair in front of screen.

Hall chair to secretary.

Pouf back to I-1 position in front of chaise.

Blue armchair on floor R. of coffee table, back lying over table.

Venetian shade stage R. window half down in "fan" position.

Windowshades stage L. windows—all almost completely down.

DUSTSHEETS:
One over chandelier.
One over sofa and coffee table.
One over center floor area.
One over secretary and hall chair.
One over sideboard (then re-set clock and seashell on top).
One over screen and secretary chair.
One over chaise, pouf and footstool and phone table.
One over dresser in bedroom.
One over hall table.

BRING ON:
Food tray with sterno stove, food tins, bowl of milk, spoon, bread and set on top of chair back on coffee table.
Dead basket of flowers (duplicate of Act II) set on hall table.

COSTUME PLOT
WOMEN

SHE
Act I—*Scene 1*

Pink dressing gown.
Gold watch.
Leather shoes.
Stockings.
Matching clutch bag.

Act I—*Scene 2*

Blue tea gown.
Gold watch (I-1).
Shoes (I-1).
Stockings (I-1).

Act II

White satin evening gown, jewel attached.
Pair blue satin gloves.
Diamond bracelet.
Pair diamond and pearl earrings.
White and gold bag.
Wedding ring.
Engagement ring.
Dinner ring.
Fur stole.

Act III

Ivory coat.
Beige dress.
Hat.
Gloves.
Taupe colored shoes.
Matching leather bag.
Gold pin.
Stockings (I-1).

ALICE
Act I—*Scene 1*

Pink tweed dress.
Green and brown sweater.
Black loafers.
Black wool stockings.

93

COSTUME PLOT

Act I—*Scene 2*

Blue sweater.
Blue slacks.
Loafers (I-1).
Blue raincoat.
Scarf.

Act II

Same as I-2, minus raincoat.

Act III

Yellow dress with jacket.
Beige stockings.
Pair brown shoes.

Act I—*Scene 1*

ROXANE
Pink wool suit with mink collar.
Pair bone colored shoes.
Stockings.
Pair white kid gloves.
Pink wool hat.

Act II

Blue organdy evening dress.
Pair blue silk shoes.
Same stockings.

Act III

Ivory wool coat.
Shoes (I-1).
Stockings (I-1).
Lace petticoat.

MEN'S COSTUME PLOT

SIR GREGORY

Act II

Black Tuxedo.
Tuxedo shirt.
Black bow tie.
White suspenders.
Cuff links.
Black socks.
Black shoes.
Black silk vest.

Act III

Brown suit.
Green brown top coat.

Cream shirt.
Brown tie.
Cuff links.
Brown hat.
Brown shoes.
Gloves, umbrella (black).
Silk scarf.
Watch fob and chain.
Socks (Act II).

BENT

Act I—*Scene 1*

Double breasted blue suit.
Striped shirt, detachable collar.
Grey tie.
Black shoes.
Watch and chain (Turnip watch).
Rose in lapel.
Steel rimmed eyeglasses.
Pair suspenders.
Dark grey top coat.
Black hat.
Cuff links.

Act I—*Scene 2*

Take off blue jacket and replace with black cotton jacket. Rest
is the same.

Act II

Butler's tails.
Black vest.
White dress shirt.
Black bow tie.
Cuff links.
White suspenders.
Soxs (I-1).
Black shoes.

Act III

Pair grey pants.
Grey sweater.
Neck band shirt without collar.
Pair suspenders (worn hanging down).
Pair old slippers.
Soxs (I-1).

TARVER

ACT I—*Scene 1*

Grey suit with vest.
Black belt.
Shirt with detachable collar.
Grey tie.
Black soxs.
Black shoes.
Cuff links.

ACT I—*Scene 2*

Greenish brown suit with vest.
Shirt with detachable collar.
Brown or maroon tie.
Black derby and umbrella.
Shoes and soxs (I-1).
Pair cuff links.

ACT II

Black tuxedo with black vest.
Dress shirt.
White suspenders.
Soxs (I-1).
Cuff links.
Black bow tie.
Black shoes.

ACT III

Green suit.
Shirt (I-1).
Tie.
Soxs, shoes, belt (I-1).
Cuff links.

OLIVER

ACT I—*Scene 1*

Tweed sport jacket.
Pair grey slacks.
Pair black soxs.
Pair black shoes.
Cream colored shirt.
Brown tie.
Cuff links.
Belt.

ACT I—*Scene 2*

Same but add:
Blue sweater.
Blue tie.

ACT II

Tuxedo with cumerbund.
White dress shirt.
Pair cuff links.
Black shoes.
Soxs (I-1).
Pair white suspenders.
Black bow tie.

ACT III

Covert suit.
Shirt (I-1).
Brown tie.
Brown soxs.
Brown loafers.
Brown belt.
Cuff links (I-1).
Tweed top coat.

THE BOXER (Red Gus Risko)

ACT I—*Scene 2*

Camel hair polo coat.
Beige sweater.
Brown slacks.
Brown shoes.
Brown gloves.
Brown soxs.
Special body padding.

ACT II

Set of tails with white vest.
White dress shirt with collar.
White bow tie.
White suspenders.
Cuff links and studs.
Black soxs.
Blacks pumps.

Act III

Navy jacket.
Navy blue sweater.
Navy wool cap.
Pair greenish pants.
Black soxs (Act II).
Pair brown shoes (I-2).

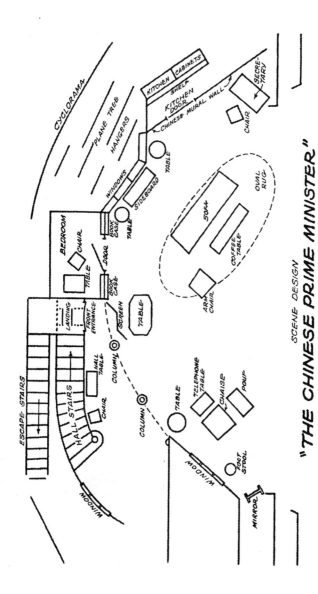

SCENE DESIGN

"THE CHINESE PRIME MINISTER"

NOTE: FRONT ENTRANCE IS DIRECTLY BELOW LANDING AT TOP OF HALL STAIRS.

OTHER TITLES AVAILABLE FROM SAMUEL FRENCH

CAPTIVE
Jan Buttram

Comedy / 2m, 1f / Interior

A hilarious take on a father/daughter relationship, this off beat comedy combines foreign intrigue with down home philosophy. Sally Pound flees a bad marriage in New York and arrives at her parent's home in Texas hoping to borrow money from her brother to pay a debt to gangsters incurred by her husband. Her elderly parents are supposed to be vacationing in Israel, but she is greeted with a shotgun aimed by her irascible father who has been left home because of a minor car accident and is not at all happy to see her. When a news report indicates that Sally's mother may have been taken captive in the Middle East, Sally's hard-nosed brother insists that she keep father home until they receive definite word, and only then will he loan Sally the money. Sally fails to keep father in the dark, and he plans a rescue while she finds she is increasingly unable to skirt the painful truths of her life. The ornery father and his loveable but slightly-dysfunctional daughter come to a meeting of hearts and minds and solve both their problems.

OTHER TITLES AVAILABLE FROM SAMUEL FRENCH

TAKE HER, SHE'S MINE
Phoebe and Henry Ephron

Comedy / 11m, 6f / Various Sets

Art Carney and Phyllis Thaxter played the Broadway roles of parents of two typical American girls enroute to college. The story is based on the wild and wooly experiences the authors had with their daughters, Nora Ephron and Delia Ephron, themselves now well known writers. The phases of a girl's life are cause for enjoyment except to fearful fathers. Through the first two years, the authors tell us, college girls are frightfully sophisticated about all departments of human life. Then they pass into the "liberal" period of causes and humanitarianism, and some into the intellectual lethargy of beatniksville. Finally, they start to think seriously of their lives as grown ups. It's an experience in growing up, as much for the parents as for the girls.

"A warming comedy. A delightful play about parents vs kids.
It's loaded with laughs. It's going to be a smash hit."
– *New York Mirror*